Heinemann is an imprint of Pearson Education Limited, a company incorporated in England and
Wales, having its registered office at Edinburgh Gate, Harlow, Essex, CM20 2JE. Registered company
number: 872828

www.heinemann.co.uk

Heinemann is a registered trademark of Pearson Education Limited

Text © Pearson Education Limited

First published 2008

12 11 10 09 08
10 9 8 7 6 5 4 3 2 1

British Library Cataloguing in Publication Data is available from the British Library on request.

ISBN 978 0 435131 95 1

Selection, introduction and activities by Sam Custance
Typeset by Phoenix Photosetting Chatham, Kent
Printed in and bound in the UK by Scotprint

Disclaimer: this collection contains some unhibited and explicit language.

Acknowledgements

Extract from *Julie and Me ... And Michael Owen Makes Three* by Alan Gibbons, published by Orion
Children's Books. Reprinted with permission of The Orion Publishing Group Limited; 'Worth
It' by Malorie Blackman. Copyright © Malorie Blackman, 1992. Reprinted by permission of A.
M. Heath & Co Ltd; extract from *The Princess Diaries* by Meg Cabot, published by Macmillan.
Copyright © Meg Cabot LLC 2000. Reprinted with permission of Macmillan; 'The Jump' by
Anthony Masters, from *Good Sports*. Copyright © Anthony Masters. Reprinted with permission of
Caroline Sheldon Literary Agency; 'The Princess Spy' by Jamila Gavin from *War: Stories Of Conflict*
published by Macmillan. Reprinted with permission of David Higham Associates Ltd; extract from
Very Different by Anne Fine, published by Egmont. Reprinted with kind permission of David Higham
Associates Limited; 'Bits of an autobiography I may not write' by Morris Gleitzman, from *Kids'
Night In*. Reprinted with permission of Penguin Australia Group Pty Ltd; extract (slightly adapted,
swear words removed only) from *The Life And Times Of The Thunderbolt Kid* by Bill Bryson, published
by Doubleday. Reprinted by permission of The Random House Group Ltd; 'Double Thirteen' by
Eleanor Updale. Copyright © 2005 by Eleanor Updale. Reproduced by permission of Felicity Bryan
Agency and the author; 'The Daughter' by Jacqueline Wilson from *Centuries of Stories*. Reprinted with
permission of David Higham Associates Ltd; 'Real Tears' by Celia Rees, from *War: Stories Of Conflict*
edited by Michael Morpurgo, published by Macmillan. © Celia Rees. Reprinted by permission of
Rosemary Sandberg Ltd; 'Mrs Bixby and the Colonel's Coat' by Roald Dahl, first published in *Kiss,
Kiss* published by Penguin Books. Reprinted with permission of David Higham Associates Ltd;
'Left Foot Forward' by Jan Mark from *Good Sports*. Reprinted with permission of David Higham
Associates Ltd; 'No Sweat' by Michelle Magorian, from *In Deep Water*. Copyright © 1992 by Michelle
Magorian, published by Viking/Puffin Books. Reprinted with permission of Rogers, Coleridge and
White Ltd; 'Going Up' by Robert Swindells, from *The Young Oxford Book of Football Stories* published
by OUP 1998. Copyright © Robert Swindells. Reprinted with permission of Jennifer Luithlen
Agency; 'A Place on the Piano' by Eva Ibbotson, from *War: Stories Of Conflict* edited by Michael
Morpurgo, published by Macmillan. Reprinted with permission of Macmillan.

Contents

Introduction

The new revised Curriculum and Programme of Study, being implemented from 2008, recommends more authors at Key Stage 3 than before. This collection features pieces by several of them, including Morris Gleitzman, Malorie Blackman, Celia Rees, Jamila Gavin, Jan Mark, Robert Swindells, Alan Gibbons, and Michelle Magorian. However, I believe a collection of short stories should also include the master of the genre, Roald Dahl, and the former Children's Laureate, Anne Fine. Among my own students, keen readers of fiction suggested Jacqueline Wilson and Meg Cabot, while more reluctant readers of fiction said they liked to read about sport, history, humour and diaries. I had to include Bill Bryson, my own favourite: I challenge anyone to read 'Schooldays' and not find it funny.

For each of the four genres there are two stories for Year 7 and two for Year 8. However, the activities are all based on the reading Assessment Foci (AFs) and the National Literacy Strategy (NLS) objectives, which are largely taken from the Text Level Reading section and are mapped for both Years 7 and 8. As this book is being published at the time of the crossover to the Renewed Framework Objectives, these have also been included in the schemes. I wanted to ensure that the scheme taught and assessed students' reading skills, which is why each genre includes a story with activities based on Assessing Pupil Progress (APP) tasks, which can be marked using the QCA marking grids.

The scheme of work includes thinking skills and guided reading tasks. Encouraging group work empowers students to talk about their reading. Word-association games encourage students to make connections between words and themes, and in turn to engage with a text before reading it, using radial diagrams to explore and extend their thoughts and Venn diagrams for comparisons and contrasts. To help analyse these texts, I have used the Point, Evidence, Explanation model, so that students can see their own development towards levels 5 and 6. Each lesson plan has differentiated activities and extension or homework tasks to enable students to develop their skills, whether they are working at level 3 or towards level 6. The lesson plans for 'Mrs Bixby and the Colonel's Coat' include guided reading cards with tasks that could be used for any short story.

I hope that you and your students enjoy studying this collection.

Sam Custance

The Gnomecoming Party
Anne Fine

Last week of term, see? So the orders are raining down. 'I want all of these lockers cleared by Friday.' 'If there's as much lost property in this cupboard next week as there is now, you lot are going to have some very irritated parents.'

Go home and it's worse. 'You realise you're going to have to *vacuum* this carpet when you've finished unloading that school junk on to it, don't you?' 'I hope you don't think you're just going to add one more archaeological layer to the rubbish already festering in that cupboard. Just clear out the whole lot and sort it properly.'

No point in arguing. So I set to and got on with it. It was like boot camp. Fresh commands kept hurtling over. 'Anything you've grown out of in this pile, please.' 'Surely at least some of these old toys could go to Oxfam? You never play with them.'

But they're still *mine*. Carefully I raised the lid of my huge box of building bits to make sure Mum hadn't been doing any secret clearing of her own. No, there they all were – shoals of brightly-coloured plastic rectangles with those knobbly bits across the top that stick them to the next piece. I scooped up a couple of handfuls to hear that sweet clattery all-the-bits-tipped-on-the-carpet-at-once sound one more time.

And that's when I found him. I saw his little pointy cap first. But when I dug my hands in deeper and fished him out, there he was, all of him: Geoffrey the Gnome.

Geoffrey the next-door's garden gnome, to be precise. I stole him years ago. Let's not get into this blame thing. I know it's wrong to steal – bleh, blehdibleh bleh, etc. – but all I intended at the start was to borrow him. Just for a morning. Then he'd have been back in the Urquharts' garden without anyone even noticing he'd been gone.

It was pottery class, see? And you don't mess with Miss Hooper. You simply do not mess with women like that. If she says she wants everybody's pottery goblin from last week's lesson back for a morning exhibition in the hall, then back it comes.

Except I'd broken mine. Well, I hadn't exactly broken him. I'd left him in the driveway with a little black home-made pit stop flag in his hand to greet my dad when he drove home from work.

'Well, what did you *expect* to happen?' he asked me as I stood forlornly staring at the crumbly bits. 'You surely didn't think I would *notice* it, did you? You can hardly have expected me to have had time to *brake?*'

'It was waving a flag,' I reminded him.

Dad picked up what was left of that. 'James, this flag is approximately two centimetres by three. I'm not in the habit of driving with night-vision binoculars moulded to my spectacles. Nor do I customarily scour the driveway for artwork as I come in.'

'All right. Keep your hair on,' I told him. 'After all, it's my pottery goblin lying there in splinters. Not yours.'

And it was me, not him, who was going to have to face Miss Hooper's killer stare in the morning. I only did what anyone of the meanest spirit and intelligence would have done. I sneaked round next door and rescued the Urquharts' precious Geoffrey from his dreary, unfulfilling life under their buddleia.

'Come on, Geoffs,' I told him. 'Time to heave your fat, flabby butt off that mushroom and be a bit of use to society.'

I mucked him up a bit. (Miss Hooper knows that I'm no good at pottery.) I shoved a few lumps of wet clay on to the ends of his fingers to make him look lumpy and second-rate. I put a paper cap on to hide the rather stylish way his hat was crumpled. And then I leaned a label with my name against him, shoved him practically out of sight at the back, and kept my fingers crossed till it was clear we'd got away with it and The Mad Potter was finally satisfied enough to let everyone take their poor derided goblin home again for a bit of peace and quiet.

Obviously, I meant to take him back next door at once. It's so long ago now, I can hardly remember what made it so awkward. That workman installing the Urquharts' new movement-sensitive security light can't have helped matters. Or that grousing over the fence. 'Now even Geoffrey's vanished! Believe me, these vandals won't get away with it next time!' I doubt if all that encouraged me to rush into being caught red-handed. I can only presume I shoved Geoffrey safely away in my big box of building bits till I felt brave enough to have a go.

Shame I forgot where I put him so quickly.

Be fair. I never left the Urquharts worrying. When the subject of Geoffrey going AWOL came up again at their boring Christmas drinks party – ('Yes, James. You *do* have to go. It's important to learn to be civil to neighbours.') – I made a real effort, writing a postcard and making Mrs Harrison at school promise faithfully she'd post it with all hers from Mallorca:

> *REALLY NEEDED A GOOD HOLIDAY AFTER*
> *ALL THOSE YEARS IN THE GARDEN. HAVING A*
> *WONDERFUL TIME. LOVE TO ALL AT NO. 27.*
> *GEOFFREY*

'Just so my uncle doesn't upset the only neighbours he forgot. This way, they'll simply think their card took longer than all the others to be delivered.'

She was a soft touch – didn't even charge me for the stamp. And since then, Geoffrey's sent the Urquharts postcards from every corner of the globe. He's quite the world traveller. Sometimes I get the local colour up the spout. They were a bit baffled when the card nattered on about sunbathing when he was in Reykjavik. And surfing in Idaho. And luxury hotels in Chad. But that was my fault, handing the cards to perfect strangers who'd missed the Gatwick Express and had to change at East Croydon. Daft of me, really. I should have stuck to what I usually did, bribing my mates at school to sneak them in with their parents' cards. After all, nothing that Geoffrey ever wrote was more of a lie than the sort of stuff they send to friends and family to cheer themselves up about wasting their money: 'Having a simply lovely time – here in Vieux Crudville. Locals so friendly. Children loving every minute.'

Well, now I'd found him. Time to give him back. He still looked natty. The lumps of clay I'd shoved all over him to fool Miss Hooper had fallen off. I reckoned he looked quite as good as before, and certainly a whole lot better than if he'd spent the intervening years with little gifts dropping on him from birds on high, and chips taken out of him each time Mr Urquhart came round the buddleia too fast on the mower.

I didn't want to give them heart attacks. So I wrote one last postcard. Before, I'd always dashed these off without much thought, like doing poems for homework. This time I sucked my pencil long and hard. And that's when the big idea flashed up. If I'd been gone for three long years, what would I want?

That's right. A party.

TO ALL MY FRIENDS AT NO. 27. PUT OUT THE BUNTING! MY TRAVELS ARE OVER. A WISER AND MORE THOUGHTFUL CREATURE

RETURNS TO HIS SPOTTED MUSHROOM –
AND YOU.

YOUR LOVING,
GEOFFREY

Good, eh? I got a man at Purley to promise to post it from Rotherhithe. Then I put up a poster in school:

GOBLIN REUNION!!! CLASS OF 1997!

Mr Hollingdale screeched to a halt in the corridor. 'So what's all this about?'

'Party,' I told him. 'Party for pottery goblins.'

He gave me one of his brain-frying stares. 'Am I to understand that, just as I begin to make headway clearing a term's detritus, you are about to encourage your year group to bring some of the least attractive *objets d'art* ever seen in my classroom back into school?'

'Party, see?' I persisted. 'Party for goblins.'

He laid his hand on my forehead. 'Feeling all right, are you, James?' he asked in that tone that implies, if you are, you soon won't be.

'No, really,' I insisted. 'We all spent hours on those goblins, and all that ever happened was that they sat for a morning on the display table in assembly, with people scoffing at them.'

He looked a little guilty. (He'd scoffed more than most.)

'So,' I said. 'I'm arranging a reunion.'

He went off then, with that strained look of his that seems to say, 'Do nothing rash. Think of your pension.' Everyone else was dead keen. Ted got his goblin back from his granny. Todwell sneaked his away from pride of place on his stepmother's mantelpiece. (My golly, that woman must try hard.) Justin found his in a welly. Lots of the rest surprisingly had theirs still knocking about, holding down attic hatches; propping open cupboard doors – that sort of thing. I was astonished to see how many of the things were staring at me from my locker by Thursday.

Miss Hooper sallies up, poison ducts fully inflated. 'Return of the Uglies, is it?' she asked, making it clear she's referring as much to us as anything stuffed in my locker. She picked up Todwell's. 'What mark did I give this?'

'B,' Tods said, filled with modest pride.

'Mistake, that,' she said, poling off again. 'Should have been a double detention.' And since she'd done her bit to sour the festive mood, that's when I broke the sad news:

'You're none of you invited, I'm afraid. This party's "Goblins Only".'

Nobody cared a jot. I was quite hurt. No time to brood, though, since it took an hour or more to drag those ugly little pottery beasts all the way up Acacia Avenue. 'Oh, not more stuff!' Mum wailed as I staggered past, weighed down with black bags, a satanic Santa.

But it was worth it. Oh, yes. It was worth it. Worth missing Thursday night's repeat of Morecambe and Wise. (When else would both the Urquharts tell themselves it was only the cat setting all the lights flashing?) Worth staying up till midnight to make the bunting, and creeping out again just before dawn to drape it all over the buddleia. Worth getting my socks scorched off later for pinching Mum's precious collection of economy-class sherry miniatures, and strewing them from the box hedge to the magnolia. Worth sneaking back and forth for half an hour with lumpy, misbegotten party animals that only a desperate stepmother would look at twice.

But, most of all, worth standing there at the window at eight o'clock, knotting my school tie for the last time that term, and seeing everything.

'Lilian! Lilian!' Mr Urquhart was rushing up and down like a madman. 'Our Geoffrey's back! It's Geoffrey! Just like the postcard said! Geoffrey!'

Mrs Urquhart appeared in her nightie. 'Really?'

'Yes, really! Look!'

And so they did. Looked at the tiny little pottery revellers flat out on their lawn. Looked at the dewsoaked banners flapping from laurel to laurel: *WELCOME HOME, GEOFFREY!* Looked at the rather tacky homemade bunting and miniature bottles strewn all around from what had obviously been the world's best homecoming party.

And, most of all, looked at Geoffrey, spruce as before, back on his spotted mushroom.

There was, I thought, a sort of reverent hush about the moments after that. Mum floated up behind me. Together we stared down at Mr and Mrs Urquhart, taking it in turns to clutch Geoffrey to their bosoms and stare in wonder at the squalor round them.

'Could this be anything to do with you?' she asked at last.

I shook my head. 'Mystery!' I assured her, carrying on knotting my tie and pulling on my socks. 'But at least it'll give them something different to talk about over the fence and at their ghastly, boring Christmas party.'

She gave me a beady look I took to mean, 'Don't think you've heard the last of this.'

But it was obviously not the time. After all, she had to get to work, and I had school. And there'll be time enough to face the music. Eight in the morning is not the perfect hour of day for long confessions, explanations and apologies.

And, today of all days, it's important to be first in the queue for assembly.

It's end of term, see? And about time too.

More Bits of an Autobiography I May Not Write

Morris Gleitzman

I'll never forget when we got our first dog. The excitement! The noise! The joyful howls (the dog). The puddles on the carpet (me).

I'd read all the books and knew exactly what to do. First, give her a feed.

'Better let us do that, Dad,' said the kids, taking the bowl. 'Better safe than sorry.'

I was indignant. The dog was indignant.

'Why?' I demanded.

'Because,' whispered the kids so the dog wouldn't hear, 'you're hopeless with pets.'

I was deeply hurt. 'That goldfish,' I retorted, 'died of a bad cold.'

The kids looked at me sternly. 'It died,' they said, 'because of what you fed it.'

I was even more indignant. 'The box had pictures of fish on it,' I said. 'How was I to know it was cat food?'

The kids looked sad. The dog looked nervous. I took her for a walk round the block.

'We'll do that,' called the kids, running to catch up. 'Better safe than sorry,'

I boiled with indignation. The dog tried to hand them the lead.

'You're not being fair,' I said. 'I've never had a single accident taking a dog for a walk round the block. Or a fruit-bat. Or a blue-tongue lizard.'

'That's right,' said the kids sadly. 'Just a mouse. What on earth possessed you to throw that stick and tell our mouse to fetch it? With a hungry cat on the loose whose dinner you'd just fed to the goldfish?'

Before I could answer; I realised I was holding an empty lead. The dog had disappeared.

We found her halfway up a lamppost, trembling with fear. The kids managed to coax her down, but only after I'd come to an agreement with them. If anything happened to the dog, they'd have me arrested.

So I enrolled us both in training and obedience classes. The dog graduated after a month, but I needed an extra six weeks.

* * * *

It was a very bright jumper.

'Absolutely you, sir,' said the menswear assistant, putting on sunglasses.

I squinted at my reflection. I looked like I'd just staggered out of an explosion in a paint factory.

'You know how computer screens have millions of colours?' continued the assistant. 'Well this jumper's got even more millions. It does suit you, sir. The greens match your complexion.'

I wore it home. Cars swerved, buses ran into each other, and a light plane made a forced landing dragged down by the temporarily blinded birds clinging to its wings.

At my place people and animals dived for cover.

'Dad,' winced the kids, shielding their eyes with thick metal baking trays. 'Take it off. All the neighbours are pulling their curtains.'

Patiently I explained how I was going to speak about my books at a school the next day and how I was terrified the students would lose interest and start talking among themselves.

'Bright colours grab people's attention,' I said. 'Look at Elton John, and fire engines.'

'Dad,' sighed the kids, shielding the goldfishes' eyes with lolly wrappers. 'If the audience cops an eyeful of that jumper they may never be able to read another word you write.'

'Rubbish,' I said. 'My readers are tough, specially round the eyeballs.'

I was right. At the school the next day I had everyone's attention from the moment I walked in. I told them all about my latest book – the characters, the themes, where they could buy it and how I'd come round and clean their car if they did. Even after I'd finished speaking I could see every pair of eyes in the room still on me.

Well, not exactly on me. More on my jumper. Then I noticed every pair of lips in the room was moving and every voice was murmuring something.

'Two million six hundred and forty-two thousand nine hundred and twenty-seven,' they were saying. 'Two million six hundred and forty-two thousand nine hundred and twenty eight…'

* * * *

Bushfire!

Tummies go wobbly at the thought. One time ours almost jumped into jelly bowls and hid in the fridge. Walls of flame, two kilometres long and a hundred metres high, roaring towards our suburb at ninety kilometres an hour!

At our place we knew the emergency drill:

1. Move to Alaska.
2. If there's not enough time for that, pack one small bag each and wait to be evacuated.

The kids were packed in minutes. 'Dad,' they yelled, 'get a move on! A few essential items into a bag! Quickly!'

'I'm doing it as fast as I can,' I protested. 'This zip won't close.'

The kids looked at my bulging bag.

'Dad,' they said, 'take the television out.'

Outside, the sky was dark with smoke. The wind flung ash against the windows. We could feel the air inside the house heating up.

The kids gave a cry of alarm. A pink liquid was dripping from the bottom of my bag.

'Oh no,' they shouted. 'The wax seals on the important family documents are melting!'

'Relax,' I said. 'It's just raspberry ripple ice-cream.'

The kids gave me a look almost as scorching as the flames four kilometres to the north.

'You said essential items,' I protested.

'Essential items,' they replied, 'means birth certificates, insurance papers, passports, important letters and family photos.'

'And Garfield slippers?' I added hopefully.

Just then the wind changed and our suburb was saved. Within a few days the only things still burning at our place were my cheeks. OK, the raspberry ripple ice-cream had been a silly choice. With only minutes to salvage my most precious possessions, I'd panicked. Next time I'd do it differently. Next time I'd pause, breathe deeply, think straight, and take the choc chip.

● ● ● ●

The kids were firm but fair.

'We want you to promise,' they said, 'to look after our polluted planet and its scarce resources and not make any more unnecessary trips in the car.'

I promised.

They opened the boot and let me out.

'Because let's face it, Dad,' they said when we'd got to our destination. 'You are pretty lazy when it comes to walking.'

I couldn't deny it so I concentrated on trying to find a parking space. Which isn't easy in a shop.

From that day, though, I did try to keep my promise. When I needed milk, or a newspaper, or socks, instead of driving I walked. And I had to admit it wasn't so bad. In fact it made getting the socks much easier because my wardrobe is quite close to the bed and it had always been a bit of a squeeze getting the car into the bedroom.

I started doing my supermarket shopping entirely on foot. (Except for one time when I was overcome with exhaustion between Frozen Foods and Breakfast Cereals and had to hitch a ride on someone's trolley.)

When I went to the cinema I left the car behind completely (not just at the ticket desk).

I went to the dentist on foot. (Well, part of the way. The kids had to carry me the last fifty metres, as usual.)

I even went to the carwash on foot. (Not such a good idea. Those rotating plastic brushes really scratch your scalp.)

I went everywhere on foot for several weeks and the kids were very proud of me. I walked down the hall to their room and they told me themselves.

I wished I could feel proud too. But I couldn't, because I knew the real reason why I wasn't making any more unnecessary trips in the car – I couldn't remember which shop I'd parked it in.

● ● ● ●

It was my first time and I was determined to do a good job. I took a deep breath, and spoke clearly into the microphone.

'Good morning, ladies and gentlemen,' I said. 'I would like to demonstrate the safety features of this Boeing 767.'

The kids looked up from their cornflakes and rolled their eyes.

'Dad,' they said. 'It's not a Boeing 767, it's a house.'

Typical. Here I was, trying to keep them safe and healthy, and all they could do was criticise.'

'If you require oxygen,' I continued, 'a mask will fall from the kitchen cupboard above your heads. Place it firmly over your nose and mouth and breathe normally, but watch you don't suck in any teaspoons.'

'Dad,' said the kids, 'look out the window. Those white blobs aren't clouds, they're Mrs Bryant's poodles. We're not thirty-six thousand feet up, we're at home.'

'Exactly,' I said. 'Eighty-seven percent of all accidents happen at home, and only zero point zero zero zero three per cent happen on planes. Why? Because on planes they take safety seriously. In case of emergency, your life jackets are located under your dining chairs.'

I watched as the kids stopped straining against their seat belts trying to reach the milk, and thought about this.

'Gee,' they said, brows furrowed, 'you've got a point.'

I gave a small triumphant smile as I pointed to the nearest exits. My plan was a success.

The Boeing 767 arrived a week later.

'Your kids ordered it,' said the second-hand plane dealer. 'But they said you'd pay. That's eighty million dollars, plus two million for delivery and mudflaps.'

I stood there, mouth open. The bowl of cornflakes I'd been eating slipped from my fingers and nearly fell on my foot.

'By the way,' said the dealer. 'I wouldn't leave it there blocking the street like that, it might cause an accident.'

I ignored him. He was just trying to sell me a hangar.

● ● ● ●

I don't know about you, but I've never been very good at watching TV while I'm being stared at. Specially by a dog with a lead in its mouth and two kids with cricket bats in theirs.

'Dad,' said the kids, 'you promised you'd take us to the park.'

'Wmpf,' agreed the dog.

'Don't talk with your mouths full,' I said, but they were right, I had promised. 'We agreed we'd go,' I reminded them, 'after I've finished watching *The Bill*.'

'But Dad,' they wailed, 'we thought you meant one episode on air, not two hundred and eighty-seven episodes on DVD.'

I sighed.

'Please,' I said, 'I'm trying to concentrate.'

I turned back to episode fifteen. Or was it sixteen? This was criminal.

'We'll go after I've finished watching *The Bill*,' I said firmly, 'and nothing you can say will make me change my mind.'

'Suit yourself,' said the kids, 'but if you don't get any exercise, you'll die.'

The park was cold and wet, but I didn't care because I took a brilliant diving catch.

'Howzat!' I yelled triumphantly through the mud.

The umpire shook his head.

'Wmpf,' he said, licking his bottom.

On the way home I decided there must be a way to combine telly and exercise and mud-free nostrils. That night I experimented.

'Who wants a Malteser?' I asked, tossing one up and swinging my table-tennis bat.

It was a big success with the kids. They quickly learned that when we had a TV dinner and there was no food on the plates, they had to leave their mouths open because I'd be chipping the peas in with a golf club and whacking the rissoles in with a squash racquet.

The dog liked it too. A few nights later, when I sliced my shot with the billiard cue and put his can of dog food through the TV screen in the middle of episode ninety-three of *The Bill*, I was sure he smiled.

Schooldays
Bill Bryson

Greenwood, my elementary school, was a wonderful old building, enormous to a small child, like a castle made of brick. Built in 1901, it stood off Grand Avenue at the far end of a street of outstandingly vast and elegant homes. The whole neighbourhood smelled lushly of old money.

Stepping into Greenwood for the first time was both the scariest and most exciting event of the first five years of my life. The front doors appeared to be about twenty times taller than normal doors, and everything inside was built to a similar imposing scale, including the teachers. Everything about it was intimidating and thrilling at once.

It was, I believe, the handsomest elementary school I have ever seen. Nearly everything in it – the cool ceramic water fountains, the polished corridors, the cloakrooms with their ancient, neatly spaced coat hooks, the giant clanking radiators with their intricate embossed patterns like iron veins, the glass-fronted cupboards, everything – had an agreeable creak of solid, classy, utilitarian venerability. This was a building made by craftsmen at a time when quality counted, and generations of devoted childhood learning suffused the air. If I hadn't had to spend so much of my time vaporizing teachers I would have adored the place.

Still, I was very fond of the building. One of the glories of life in that ancient lost world of the mid-twentieth century was that facilities designed for kids often were just smaller versions of things in the adult world. You can't imagine how much more splendid this made them. Our Little League baseball field, for instance, was a proper ballpark, with a grandstand and a concession stand

and press box, and real dugouts that were, as the name demands, partly subterranean (and never mind that they filled with puddles every time it rained and that the shorter players couldn't see over the edge and so tended to cheer at the wrong moments). When you ran up those three sagging steps and out on to the field you could seriously imagine that you were in Yankee Stadium. Superior infrastructure makes for richer fantasies, believe me. Greenwood contained all that in spades.

It had, for one thing, an auditorium that was just like a real theatre, with a stage with curtains and spotlights and dressing rooms behind. So however bad your school productions were – and ours were always extremely bad, partly because we had no talent and partly because Mrs De Voto, the music teacher, was a bit ancient and often nodded off at the piano – it felt like you were part of a well-ordered professional undertaking (even when you were standing there holding a long note, waiting for Mrs De Voto's chin to touch the keyboard, an event that always jerked her back into action with rousing gusto at exactly the spot where she had left off a minute or two before).

Greenwood also had the world's finest gymnasium. It was upstairs at the back of the school, which gave it a nicely unexpected air. When you opened the door, you expected to find an ordinary classroom and instead you had – hey! whoa! – a gigantic cubic vault of polished wood. It was a space to savour: it had cathedral-sized windows, a ceiling that no ball could ever reach, acres of varnished wood that had been mellowed into a honeyed glow by decades of squeaky sneakers and gentle drops of childish perspiration, and smartly echoing acoustics that made every bouncing ball sound deftly handled and seriously athletic. When the weather was good and we were sent outdoors to play, the route to the playground took us out on to a rickety metal fire escape that was unnervingly but grandly lofty. The view from the summit took in miles of rooftops and sunny countryside reaching practically to Missouri, or so it seemed.

Mostly we played indoors, however, because it was nearly always winter outside. Of course winters in those days, as with all winters of childhood, were much longer, snowier and more frigid than now. We used to get up to eleven feet of snow at a time – we seldom got less, in fact – and weeks of arctic weather so bitter you could pee icicles.

In consequence, they used to keep the school heated to roughly the temperature of the inside of a pottery kiln, so pupils and teachers alike existed in a state of permanent, helpless drowsiness. But at the same time the close warmth made everything deliciously cheery and cosy. Even Lumpy Kowalski's daily plop in his pants smelled oven-baked and kind of strangely lovely. (For six months of the year, his pants actually steamed.) On the other hand, the radiators were so hot that if you carelessly leaned an elbow on them you could leave flesh behind. The most infamous radiator-based activity was of course to pee on a radiator in one of the boys' bathrooms. This created an enormous sour stink that permeated whole wings of the school for days on end and could not be got rid of through any amount of scrubbing or airing. For this reason, anyone caught peeing on a radiator was summarily executed.

The school day was largely taken up with putting on or taking off clothing. It was an exhaustingly tedious process. It took most of the morning to take off your outdoor wear and most of the afternoon to get it back on, assuming you could find any of it among the jumbled, shifting heap of garments that carpeted the cloakroom floor to a depth of about three feet. Changing time was always like a scene at a refugee camp, with at least three kids wandering around weeping copiously because they had only one boot or no mittens. Teachers were never to be seen at such moments.

Boots in those days had strange, uncooperative clasps that managed to pinch and lacerate at the same time, producing some really interesting injuries, especially when your hands were numb with cold. The manufacturers might just as well have fashioned the clasps out of razor blades. Because they were so lethal, you ended up leaving the clasps undone, which was more macho but also let in large volumes of snow, so that you spent much of the day in sopping wet socks, which then became three times longer than your feet. In consequence of being constantly damp and hyperthermic, all children had running noses from October to April, which most of them treated as a kind of drip feeder.

Greenwood had no cafeteria, so everybody had to go home for lunch, which meant that we had to dress and undress four times in every school day – six if the teacher was foolish enough to include an outdoor recess at some point. My dear, dim friend Buddy Doberman spent so much of his life changing that he often lost track and would have to ask me whether we were putting hats on or off now. He was always most grateful for guidance.

Among the many thousands of things moms never quite understand – the manliness implicit in grass stains, the satisfaction of a really good burp or other gaseous eructation, the need from time to time to blow into straws as well as suck out of them – winter dressing has always been perhaps the most tragically conspicuous. All moms in the Fifties lived in dread of cold fronts slipping in from Canada, and therefore insisted that their children wear enormous quantities of insulating clothes for at least seven months of the year. This came mostly in the form of underwear – cotton underwear, flannel underwear, long underwear, thermal underwear, quilted underwear, ribbed underwear, underwear with padded shoulders, and possibly more; there was a lot of underwear in America in the 1950s – so that you couldn't possibly perish during any of the ten minutes you spent outdoors each day.

What they failed to take into account was that you were so mummified by extra clothing that you had no limb flexion whatever, and if you fell over you would never get up again unless someone helped you, which was not a thing you could count on. Layered underwear also made going to the bathroom an unnerving challenge. The manufacturers did put an angled vent in every item, but these never quite matched up, and anyway if your penis is only the size of a newly budded acorn it's asking a lot to thread it through seven or eight layers of underwear and still maintain a competent handhold. In any visit to the restroom, you would hear at least one cry of anguish from someone who had lost purchase in mid–flow and was now delving frantically for the missing appendage.

Mothers also failed to realize that certain clothes at certain periods of your life would get you beaten up. If, for instance, you wore snowpants beyond the age of six, you got beaten up for it. If you wore a hat with ear flaps or, worse, a chin strap, you could be sure of a beating, or at the very least a couple of scoops of snow down your back. The wimpiest, most foolish thing of all was to wear galoshes. Galoshes were unstylish and ineffective and even the name just sounded stupid and inescapably humiliating. If your mom made you wear galoshes at any point in the year, it was a death sentence. I knew kids who couldn't get prom dates in high school because every girl they asked remembered that they had worn galoshes in third grade.

I was not a popular pupil with the teachers. Only Mrs De Voto liked me, and she liked all the children, largely because she didn't know who any of them were. She wrote 'Billy sings with enthusiasm' on all my report cards, except once or twice when she wrote 'Bobby sings with enthusiasm'. But I excused her for that because she was kind and well meaning and smelled nice.

The other teachers – all women, all spinsters – were large, lumpy, suspicious, frustrated, dictatorial and unkind. They smelled peculiar, too – a mixture of camphor, mentholated mints and the curious belief (which may well have contributed to their spinsterhood) that a generous dusting of powder was as good as a bath. Some of these women had been powdering up for years and believe me it didn't work.

They insisted on knowing strange things, which I found bewildering. If you asked to go to the restroom, they wanted to know whether you intended to do Number 1 or Number 2, a curiosity that didn't strike me as entirely healthy. Besides, these were not terms used in our house. In our house, you either went toity or had a BM (for bowel movement), but mostly you just went 'to the bathroom' and made no public declarations with regard to intent. So I hadn't the faintest idea, the first time I requested permission to go, what the teacher meant when she asked me if I was going to do Number 1 or Number 2.

'Well, I don't know,' I replied frankly and in a clear voice. 'I need to do a big BM. It could be as much as a three or a four.'

I got sent to the cloakroom for that. I got sent to the cloakroom a lot, often for reasons that I didn't entirely understand, but I never really minded. It was a curious punishment, after all, to be put in a place where you were alone with all your classmates' snack foods and personal effects and no one could see what you were getting into. It was also a very good time to get some private reading done.

As a scholar, I made little impact. My very first report card, for the first semester of first grade, had just one comment from the teacher: 'Billy talks in a low tone.' That was it. Nothing about my character or deportment, my sure touch with phonics, my winning smile or can-do attitude, just a terse and enigmatic 'Billy talks in a low tone.' It wasn't even possible to tell whether it was a complaint or just an observation. After the second semester, the report said: 'Billy still talks in a low tone.' All my other report cards – every last one, apart from Mrs De Voto's faithful recording of my enthusiastic noise-making – had blanks in the comment section. It was as if I wasn't there. In fact, often I wasn't.

Kindergarten, my debut experience at Greenwood, ran for just half a day. You attended either the morning session or the afternoon session. I was assigned to the afternoon group, which was a lucky thing because I didn't get up much before noon in those days. (We were night owls in our house.) One of my very first experiences of kindergarten was arriving for the afternoon, keen to get cracking with the fingerpaints, and being instructed to lie down on a little rug for a nap. Resting was something we had to do a lot of in the Fifties; I presume that it was somehow attached to the belief that it would thwart polio. But as I had only just risen to come to school, it seemed a little eccentric to be lying down again. The next year was even worse because we were expected to turn up at 8.45 in the morning, which was not a time I chose to be active.

My best period was the late evening. I liked to watch the ten o'clock news with Russ Van Dyke, the world's best television newsman (better even than Walter Cronkite), and then *Sea Hunt* starring Lloyd Bridges (some genius at KRNT-TV decided 10.30 at night was a good time to run a show enjoyed by children, which was correct) before settling down with a largish stack of comic books. I was seldom asleep much before midnight, so when my mother called me in the morning, I usually found it inconvenient to rise. So I didn't go to school if I could help it.

I probably wouldn't have gone at all if it hadn't been for mimeograph paper. Of all the tragic losses since the 1950s, mimeograph paper may be the greatest. With its rapturously fragrant, sweetly aromatic pale blue ink, mimeograph paper was literally intoxicating. Two deep draughts of a freshly run-off mimeograph worksheet and I would be the education system's willing slave for up to seven hours. Go to any crack house and ask the people where their dependency problems started and they will tell you, I'm certain, that it was with mimeograph paper in second grade. I used to bound out of bed on a Monday morning because that was the day that fresh mimeographed worksheets were handed out. I draped them over my face and drifted off to a private place where fields were green, everyone went barefoot and the soft trill of pan pipes floated on the air. But most of the rest of the week I either straggled in around mid-morning, or didn't come in at all. I'm afraid the teachers took this personally.

They were never going to like me anyway. There was something about me – my dreaminess and hopeless forgetfulness, my lack of button-cuteness, my permanent default expression of pained dubiousness – that rubbed them the wrong way. They disliked all children, of course, particularly little boys, but of the children they didn't like I believe they especially favoured me. I always did everything wrong. I forgot to bring official forms back on time. I forgot to bring cookies for class parties and Christmas cards and valentines on the appropriate festive days. I always turned up empty-handed for show and tell. I remember once in kindergarten, in a kind of desperation, I just showed my fingers.

If we were going on a school trip, I never remembered to bring a permission note from home, even after being reminded daily for weeks. So on the day of the trip everybody would have to sit moodily on the bus for an interminable period while the principal's secretary tried to track my mother down to get her consent over the phone. But my mother was always out to coffee. The whole women's department was always out to coffee. If they weren't out to coffee, they were out to lunch. It's a miracle they ever got a section out, frankly. The secretary would eventually look at me with a sad smile and we would have to face the fact together that I wasn't going to go.

So the bus would depart without me and I would spend the day in the school library, which I actually didn't mind at all. It's not as if I were missing a trip to the Grand Canyon or Cape Canaveral. This was Des Moines. There were only two places schools went on trips in Des Moines – to the Wonder Bread factory on Second Avenue and University, where you could watch freshly made bread products travelling round an enormous room on conveyor belts under the very light supervision of listless drones in paper hats (and you could be excused for thinking that the purpose of school visits was to give the drones something to stare at), and the museum of the Iowa State Historical Society, the world's quietest and most uneventful building, where you discovered that not a great deal had ever happened in Iowa; nothing at all if you excluded ice ages.

A more regular humiliation was forgetting to bring money for savings stamps. Savings stamps were like savings bonds, but bought a little at a time. You gave the teacher twenty or thirty cents (two dollars if your dad was a lawyer, surgeon or orthodontist) and she gave you a commensurate number of patriotic-looking stamps – one for each dime spent – which you then licked and placed over stamp-sized squares in a savings stamp book. When you had filled a book, you had $10 worth of savings and America was that much closer to licking Communism. I can still see the stamps now: they were a pinkish red with a picture of a minuteman with a three-cornered hat, a musket and a look of resolve. It was a sacred patriotic duty to buy savings stamps.

One day each week – I couldn't tell you which one now; I couldn't tell you which one then – Miss Grumpy or Miss Lesbos or Miss Squat Little Fat Thing would announce that it was time to collect money for US Saving Stamps and every child in the classroom but me would immediately reach into their desk or schoolbag and extract a white envelope containing money and join a line at the teacher's desk. It was a weekly miracle to me that all these other pupils *knew* on which day they were supposed to bring money and then actually *remembered* to do so. That was at least one step of sharpness too many for a Bryson.

One year I had four stamps in my book (two of them pasted in upside down); in all the other years I had zero. My mother and I between us had not remembered once. The Butter boys all had more stamps than I did. Each year the teacher held up my pathetically barren book as an example for all the other pupils of how not to support your country and they would all laugh – that peculiar braying laugh that exists only when children are invited by adults to enjoy themselves at the expense of another child. It is the cruellest laugh in the world.

Despite these self-inflicted hardships, I quite enjoyed school, especially reading. We were taught to read from Dick and Jane books, solid hardbacks bound in a heavy-duty red or blue fabric. They had short sentences in large type and lots of handsome watercolour illustrations featuring a happy, prosperous, good-looking, law-abiding but interestingly strange family. In the Dick and Jane books, Father is always called Father, never Dad or Daddy, and always wears a suit, even for Sunday lunch – even, indeed, to drive to Grandfather and Grandmother's farm for a weekend visit. Mother is always Mother. She is always on top of things, always nicely groomed in a clean frilly apron. The family have no last name. They live in a pretty house with a picket fence on a pleasant street, but they have no radio or TV and their bathroom has no toilet (so no problems deciding between Number 1 and Number 2 in *their* household). The children – Dick, Jane and little Sally – have only the simplest and most timeless of toys: a ball, a wagon, a kite, a wooden sailboat.

No one ever shouts or bleeds or weeps helplessly. No meals ever burn, no drinks ever spill (or intoxicate). No dust accumulates. The sun always shines. The dog never shits on the lawn. There are no atomic bombs, no Butter boys, no cicada killers. Everyone is at all times clean, healthy, strong, reliable, hard-working, American and white.

Every Dick and Jane story provided some simple but important lesson – respect your parents, share your possessions, be polite, be honest, be helpful, and above all work hard. Work, according to *Growing Up with Dick and Jane,* was the eighteenth new word we learned. I'm amazed it took them that long. Work was what you did in our world.

I was captivated by the Dick and Jane family. They were so wonderfully, fascinatingly different from my own family. I particularly recall one illustration in which all the members of the Dick and Jane family, for entertainment, stand on one leg, hold the other out straight and try to grab a toe on the extended foot without losing balance and falling over. They are having the most wonderful time doing this. I stared and stared at that picture and realized that there were no circumstances, including at gunpoint, in which you could get all the members of my family to try to do that together.

Because our Dick and Jane books at Greenwood were ten or fifteen years old, they depicted a world that was already gone. The cars were old-fashioned, the buses too. The shops the family frequented were of a type that no longer existed – pet shops with puppies in the window, toy stores with wooden toys, grocers where items were fetched for you by a cheerful man in a white apron. I found everything about this enchanting. There was no dirt or pain in their world. They could even go into Grandfather's hen house to collect eggs and not gag from the stink or become frantically attached to a blob of chicken shit. It was a wonderful world, a perfect world, friendly, hygienic, safe, better than real. There was just one very odd thing about the Dick and Jane books. Whenever any of the characters spoke, they didn't sound like humans.

'Here we are at the farm,' says Father in a typical passage as he bounds from the car (dressed, not incidentally, in a brown suit), then adds a touch robotically: 'Hello, Grandmother. Here we are at the farm.'

'Hello,' responds Grandmother. 'See who is here. It is my family. Look, look! Here is my family.'

'Oh, look! Here we are at the farm,' adds Dick, equally amazed to find himself in a rural setting inhabited by loved ones. He, too, seems to have a kind of mental stuck needle. 'Here we are at the farm,' he goes on. 'Here is Grandfather, too! Here we are at the farm.'

It was like this on every page. Every character talked exactly like people whose brains had been taken away. This troubled me for a long while. One of the great influences of my life in this period was the movie *Invasion of the Body Snatchers,* which I found so convincingly scary that I took it as more or less real, and for about three years I watched my parents extremely closely for tell-tale signs that they had been taken over by alien life forms them-selves, before eventually realizing that it would be impossible to tell if they had been; that indeed the first clue that they were turning into pod people would be their becoming *more normal* – and I wondered for a long time if the Dick and Jane family (or actually, for I wasn't completely stupid, the creators of the

Dick and Jane family) had been snatched and were now trying to soften us up for a podding of our own. It made sense to me.

I loved the Dick and Jane books so much that I took them home and kept them. (There were stacks of spares in the cloakroom.) I still have them and still look at them from time to time. And I am still looking for a family that would all try to touch their toes together.

Once I had the Dick and Jane books at home and could read them at my leisure, over a bowl of ice cream or while keeping half an eye on the television, I didn't see much need to go to school. So I didn't much go. By second grade I was pretty routinely declining my mother's daily entreaties to rise. It exasperated her to the point of two heavy sighs and some speechless clucking – as close to furious as she ever got – but I realized quite early on that if I just went completely limp and unresponsive and assumed a posture of sacklike uncooperativeness, stirring only very slightly from time to time to mumble that I was really quite seriously unwell and needed rest, she would eventually give up and go away, saying, 'Your dad would be *furious* if he was here now'.

But the thing was he wasn't there. He was in Iowa City or Columbus or San Francisco or Sarasota. He was always somewhere. As a consequence he only learned of these matters twice a year when he was given my report card to review and sign. These always became occasions in which my mother was in as much trouble as I was.

'How can he have 26¼ absences in one semester?' he would say in pained dismay. 'And how, come to that, do you get a quarter of an absence?' He would look at my mother in further pained dismay. 'Do you just send part of him to school sometimes? Do you keep his legs at home?'

My mother would make small fretful noises that didn't really amount to speech.

'I just don't get it,' my father would go on, staring at the report card as if it were a bill for damages unfairly rendered. 'It's gotten beyond a joke. I really think the only solution is a military academy.'

My father had a strange, deep attraction to military academies. The idea of permanent, systematized punishment appealed to a certain dark side of his character. Large numbers of these institutions advertised at the back of the *National Geographic* – why there I don't know – and I would often find those pages bookmarked by him. The ads always showed a worried-looking boy in grey military dress, a rifle many times too big for him at his shoulder, above a message saying something like:

Camp Hardship Military Academy
TEACHING BOYS TO KILL SINCE 1867
We specialize in building character and
eliminating pansy traits.
Write for details at PO Box 1,
Chicken Gizzard, Tenn.

It never came to anything. He would write off for a leaflet – my father was a fiend for leaflets of all types, and catalogues too if they were free – and find out that the fees were as much as for an Austin Healey sports car or a trip to Europe and drop the whole notion, as one might drop a very hot platter. Anyway, I wasn't convinced that military academies were such a bad thing. The idea of being at a place where rifles, bayonets and explosives were at the core of the curriculum had a distinct appeal.

Once a month we had a civil defence drill at school. A siren would sound – a special urgent siren that denoted that this was not a fire drill or storm alert but a nuclear attack by agents of the dark forces of Communism – and everyone would scramble out of their seats and get under their desks with hands folded over heads in the nuclear attack brace position. I must have missed a few of these, for the first time one occurred in my presence I had no idea what was going on and sat fascinated as everyone around me dropped to the floor and parked themselves like little cars under their desks.

'What is this?' I asked Buddy Doberman's butt, for that was the only part of him still visible.

'Atomic bomb attack,' came his voice, slightly muffled. 'But it's OK. It's only a practice, I think!'

I remember being profoundly amazed that anyone would suppose that a little wooden desk would provide a safe haven in the event of an atomic bomb being dropped on Des Moines. But evidently they all took the matter seriously for even the teacher, Miss Squat Little Fat Thing, was inserted under her desk, too – or at least as much of her as she could get under, which was perhaps 40 per cent. Once I realized that no one was watching, I elected not to take part. I already knew how to get under a desk and was confident that this was not a skill that would ever need refreshing. Anyway, what were the chances that the Soviets would bomb Des Moines? I mean, come on.

Some weeks later I aired this point conversationally to my father while we were dining together in the Jefferson Hotel in Iowa City on one of our occasional weekends away, and he responded with a strange chuckle that Omaha, just eighty miles to the west of Des Moines, was the headquarters of Strategic Air Command, from which all American operations would be directed in the event of war. SAC would be hit by everything the Soviets could throw at it, which of course was a great deal. We in Des Moines would be up to our backsides in fallout within ninety minutes if the wind was blowing to the east, my father told me. 'You'd be dead before bedtime,' he added brightly. 'We all would'.

I don't know which I found more disturbing – that I was at grave risk in a way that I hadn't known about or that my father found the prospect of our annihilation so amusing – but either way it confirmed me in the conviction that nuclear drills were pointless. Life was too short and we'd all be dead anyway. The time would be better spent apologetically but insistently touching Mary O'Leary's budding chest. In any case, I ceased to take part in the drills.

So it was perhaps a little unfortunate that on the morning of my third or fourth drill, Mrs Unnaturally Enormous Bosom, the principal, accompanied by a man in a military uniform from the Iowa Air National Guard, made an inspection tour of the school and espied me sitting alone at my desk reading a comic adventure featuring the Human Torch and that shapely minx Asbestos Lady, surrounded by a roomful of abandoned desks, each sprouting a pair of backward-facing feet and a child's ass.

Boy, was I in trouble. In fact, it was worse than just being straightforwardly in trouble. For one thing, Miss Squat Little Fat Thing was also in trouble for having failed in her supervisory responsibilities and so became deeply, irremediably pissed off with me, and would for ever remain so.

My own disgrace was practically incalculable. I had embarrassed the school. I had embarrassed the principal. I had shamed myself. I had insulted my nation. To be cavalier about nuclear preparedness was only half a step away from treason. I was beyond hope really. Not only did I talk in a low tone, miss lots of school, fail to buy savings stamps and occasionally turn up wearing girlie Capri pants, but clearly I came from a Bolshevik household. I spent more or less the rest of my elementary school career in the cloakroom.

Mrs Bixby and the Colonel's Coat
Roald Dahl

America is the land of opportunities for women. Already they own about eighty-five per cent of the wealth of the nation. Soon they will have it all. Divorce has become a lucrative process, simple to arrange and easy to forget; and ambitious females can repeat it as often as they please and parlay their winnings to astronomical figures. The husband's death also brings satisfactory rewards and some ladies prefer to rely upon this method. They know that the waiting period will not be unduly protracted, for overwork and hypertension are bound to get the poor devil before long, and he will die at his desk with a bottle of Benzedrines in one hand and a packet of tranquillizers in the other.

Succeeding generations of youthful American males are not deterred in the slightest by this terrifying pattern of divorce and death. The higher the divorce rate climbs, the more eager they become. Young men marry like mice, almost before they have reached the age of puberty, and a large proportion of them have at least two ex-wives on the payroll by the time they are thirty-six years old. To support these ladies in the manner to which they are accustomed, the men must work like slaves, which is of course precisely what they are. But now at last, as they approach their premature middle age, a sense of disillusionment and fear begins to creep slowly into their hearts, and in the evenings they take to huddling together in little groups, in clubs and bars, drinking their whiskies and swallowing their pills, and trying to comfort one another with stories.

The basic theme of these stories never varies. There are always three main characters – the husband, the wife, and the dirty dog.

The husband is a decent clean-living man, working hard at his job. The wife is cunning, deceitful, and lecherous, and she is invariably up to some sort of jiggery-pokery with the dirty dog. The husband is too good a man even to suspect her. Things look black for the husband. Will the poor man ever find out? Must he be a cuckold for the rest of his life? Yes, he must. But wait! Suddenly, by a brilliant manoeuvre, the husband completely turns the tables on his monstrous spouse. The woman is flabbergasted, stupefied, humiliated, defeated. The audience of men around the bar smiles quietly to itself and takes a little comfort from the fantasy.

There are many of these stories going around, these wonderful wishful thinking dreamworld inventions of the unhappy male, but most of them are too fatuous to be worth repeating, and far too fruity to be put down on paper. There is one, however, that seems to be superior to the rest, particularly as it has the merit of being true. It is extremely popular with twice- or thrice-bitten males in search of solace, and if you are one of them, and if you haven't heard it before, you may enjoy the way it comes out. The story is called 'Mrs Bixby and the Colonel's Coat', and it goes something like this:

Mr and Mrs Bixby lived in a smallish apartment somewhere in New York City. Mr Bixby was a dentist who made an average income. Mrs Bixby was a big vigorous woman with a wet mouth. Once a month, always on Friday afternoons, Mrs Bixby would board the train at Pennsylvania Station and travel to Baltimore to visit her old aunt. She would spend the night with the aunt and return to New York on the following day in time to cook supper for her husband. Mr Bixby accepted this arrangement good-naturedly. He knew that Aunt Maude lived in Baltimore, and that his wife was very fond of the old lady, and certainly it would be unreasonable to deny either of them the pleasure of a monthly meeting.

'Just so long as you don't ever expect me to accompany you,' Mr Bixby had said in the beginning.

'Of course not, darling,' Mrs Bixby had answered. 'After all, she is not *your* aunt. She's mine.'

So far so good.

As it turned out, however, the aunt was little more than an alibi for Mrs Bixby. The dirty dog, in the shape of a gentleman known as the Colonel, was lurking slyly in the background, and our heroine spent the greater part of her Baltimore time in this scoundrel's company. The Colonel was exceedingly wealthy. He lived in a charming house on the outskirts of town. No wife or family encumbered him, only a few discreet and loyal servants, and in Mrs Bixby's absence he consoled himself by riding his horses and hunting the fox.

Year after year, this pleasant alliance between Mrs Bixby and the Colonel continued without a hitch. They met so seldom – twelve times a year is not much when you come to think of it – that there was little or no chance of their growing bored with one another. On the contrary, the long wait between meetings only made the heart grow fonder, and each separate occasion became an exciting reunion.

'Tally-ho!' the Colonel would cry each time he met her at the station in the big car. 'My dear, I'd almost forgotten how ravishing you looked. Let's go to earth.'

Eight years went by.

It was just before Christmas, and Mrs Bixby was standing on the station in Baltimore waiting for the train to take her back to New York. This particular visit which had just ended had been more than usually agreeable, and she was in a cheerful mood. But then the Colonel's company always did that to her these days. The man had a way of making her feel that she was altogether a rather remarkable woman, a person of subtle and exotic talents, fascinating beyond measure; and what a very different thing that was from the dentist husband at home who never succeeded in making her feel that she was anything but a sort of eternal patient, someone who dwelt in the waiting-room, silent among the magazines, seldom if ever nowadays to be called in to suffer the finicky precise ministrations of those clean pink hands.

'The Colonel asked me to give you this,' a voice beside her said. She turned and saw Wilkins, the Colonel's groom, a small wizened dwarf with grey skin, and he was pushing a large flattish cardboard box into her arms.

'Good gracious me!' she cried, all of a flutter. 'My heavens, what an enormous box! What is it, Wilkins? Was there a message? Did he send me a message?'

'No message,' the groom said, and he walked away.

As soon as she was on the train, Mrs Bixby carried the box into the privacy of the Ladies' Room and locked the door. How exciting this was! A Christmas present from the Colonel. She started to undo the string. 'I'll bet it's a dress,' she said aloud. 'It might even be two dresses. Or it might be a whole lot of beautiful underclothes. I won't look. I'll just feel around and try to guess what it is. I'll try to guess the colour as well, and exactly what it looks like. Also how much it cost.'

She shut her eyes tight and slowly lifted off the lid. Then she put one hand down into the box. There was some tissue paper on top; she could feel it and hear it rustling. There was also an envelope or a card of some sort. She ignored this and began burrowing underneath the tissue paper, the fingers reaching out delicately, like tendrils.

'My God,' she cried suddenly. 'It can't be true!'

She opened her eyes wide and stared at the coat. Then she pounced on it and lifted it out of the box. Thick layers of fur made a lovely noise against the tissue paper as they unfolded, and when she held it up and saw it hanging to its full length, it was so beautiful it took her breath away.

Never had she seen mink like this before. It *was* mink, wasn't it? Yes, of course it was. But what a glorious colour! The fur was almost pure black. At first she thought it *was* black; but when she held it closer to the window she saw that there was a touch of blue in it as well, a deep rich blue, like cobalt. Quickly she looked at the label. It said simply, WILD LABRADOR MINK. There was nothing else, no sign of where it had been bought or anything. But that, she told herself, was probably the Colonel's doing. The wily old fox was making darn sure he didn't leave any tracks. Good for him. But what in the world could it have cost? She hardly dared to think. Four, five, six thousand dollars? Possibly more.

She just couldn't take her eyes off it. Nor, for that matter, could she wait to try it on. Quickly she slipped off her own plain red coat. She was panting a little now, she couldn't help it, and her eyes were stretched very wide. But oh God, the feel of that fur! And those huge wide sleeves with their thick turned-up cuffs! Who was it had once told her that they always used female skins for the arms and male skins for the rest of the coat? Someone had told her that. Joan Rutfield, probably; though how *Joan* would know anything about *mink* she couldn't imagine.

The great black coat seemed to slide on to her almost of its own accord, like a second skin. Oh boy! It was the queerest feeling! She glanced into the mirror. It was fantastic. Her whole personality had suddenly changed completely. She looked dazzling, radiant, rich, brilliant, voluptuous, all at the same time. And the sense of power that it gave her! In this coat she could walk into any place she wanted and people would come scurrying around her like rabbits. The whole thing was just too wonderful for words!

Mrs Bixby picked up the envelope that was still lying in the box. She opened it and pulled out the Colonel's letter:

I once heard you saying you were fond of mink so I got you this. I'm told it's a good one. Please accept it with my sincere good wishes as a parting gift. For my own personal reasons I shall not be able to see you any more. Good-bye and good luck.

Well!

Imagine that!

Right out of the blue, just when she was feeling so happy.

No more Colonel.

What a dreadful shock.

She would miss him enormously.

Slowly, Mrs Bixby began stroking the lovely soft black fur of the coat.

What you lose on the swings you get back on the round-abouts.

She smiled and folded the letter, meaning to tear it up and throw it out of the window, but in folding it she noticed that there was something written on the other side:

PS Just tell them that nice generous aunt of yours gave it to you for Christmas.

Mrs Bixby's mouth, at that moment stretched wide in a silky smile, snapped back like a piece of elastic.

'The man must be mad!' she cried. 'Aunt Maude doesn't have that sort of money. She couldn't possibly give me this.'

But if Aunt Maude didn't give it to her, then who did?

Oh God! In the excitement of finding the coat and trying it on, she had completely overlooked this vital aspect.

In a couple of hours she would be in New York. Ten minutes after that she would be home, and the husband would be there to greet her; and even a man like Cyril, dwelling as he did in a dark phlegmy world of root canals, bicuspids, and caries, would start asking a few questions if his wife suddenly waltzed in from a week-end wearing a six-thousand-dollar mink coat.

You know what I think, she told herself. I think that goddamn Colonel has done this on purpose just to torture me. He knew perfectly well Aunt Maude didn't have enough money to buy this. He knew I wouldn't be able to keep it.

But the thought of parting with it now was more than Mrs Bixby could bear.

'I've *got* to have this coat!' she said aloud. 'I've got to have this coat! I've got to have this coat!'

Very well, my dear. You shall have the coat. But don't panic. Sit still and keep calm and start thinking. You're a clever girl, aren't you? You've fooled him before. The man never has been able to see much further than the end of his own probe, you know that. So just sit absolutely still and *think*. There's lots of time.

Two and a half hours later, Mrs Bixby stepped off the train at Pennsylvania Station and walked quietly to the exit. She was wearing her old red coat again now and carrying the cardboard box in her arms. She signalled for a taxi.

'Driver,' she said, 'would you know of a pawnbroker that's still open around here?'

The man behind the wheel raised his brows and looked back at her, amused.

'Plenty along Sixth Avenue,' he answered.

'Stop at the first one you see, then, will you please?' She got in and was driven away.

Soon the taxi pulled up outside a shop that had three brass balls hanging over the entrance.

'Wait for me, please,' Mrs Bixby said to the driver, and she got out of the taxi and entered the shop.

There was an enormous cat crouching on the counter eating fishheads out of a white saucer. The animal looked up at Mrs Bixby with bright yellow eyes, then looked away again and went on eating. Mrs Bixby stood by the counter, as far away from the cat as possible, waiting for someone to come, staring at the watches, the shoe buckles, the enamel brooches, the old binoculars, the broken spectacles, the false teeth. Why did they always pawn their teeth, she wondered.

'Yes?' the proprietor said, emerging from a dark place in the back of the shop.

'Oh, good evening,' Mrs Bixby said. She began to untie the string around the box. The man went up to the cat and started stroking it along the top of its back, and the cat went on eating the fishheads.

'Isn't it silly of me?' Mrs Bixby said. 'I've gone and lost my pocket-book, and this being Saturday, the banks are all closed until Monday and I've simply got to have some money for the weekend. This is quite a valuable coat, but I'm not asking much. I only want to borrow enough on it to tide me over till Monday. Then I'll come back and redeem it.'

The man waited, and said nothing. But when she pulled out the mink and allowed the beautiful thick fur to fall over the counter, his eyebrows went up and he drew his hand away from the cat and came over to look at it. He picked it up and held it out in front of him.

'If only I had a watch on me or a ring,' Mrs Bixby said, 'I'd give you that instead. But the fact is I don't have a thing with me other than this coat.' She spread out her fingers for him to see.

'It looks new,' the man said, fondling the soft fur.

'Oh yes, it is. But, as I said, I only want to borrow enough to tide me over till Monday. How about fifty dollars?'

'I'll loan you fifty dollars.'

'It's worth a hundred times more than that, but I know you'll take good care of it until I return.'

The man went over to a drawer and fetched a ticket and placed it on the counter. The ticket looked like one of those labels you tie on to the handle of your suitcase, the same shape and size exactly, and the same stiff brownish paper. But it was perforated across the middle so that you could tear it in two, and both halves were identical.

'Name?' he asked.

'Leave that out. And the address.'

She saw the man pause, and she saw the nib of the pen hovering over the dotted line, waiting.

'You don't *have* to put the name and address, do you?'

The man shrugged and shook his head and the pen-nib moved down to the next line.

'It's just that I'd rather not,' Mrs Bixby said. 'It's purely personal.'

'You'd better not lose this ticket, then.'

'I won't lose it.'

'You realize that anyone who gets hold of it can come in and claim the article?'

'Yes, I know that.'

'Simply on the number.'

'Yes. I know.'

'What do you want me to put for a description?'

'No description either, thank you. It's not necessary. Just put the amount I'm borrowing.'

The pen-nib hesitated again, hovering over the dotted line beside the word ARTICLE.

'I think you ought to put a description. A description is always a help if you want to sell the ticket. You never know, you might want to sell it sometime.'

'I don't want to sell it.'

'You might have to. Lots of people do.'

'Look,' Mrs Bixby said. 'I'm not broke, if that's what you mean. I simply lost my purse. Don't you understand?'

'You have it your own way then,' the man said. 'It's your coat.'

At this point an unpleasant thought struck Mrs Bixby. 'Tell me something,' she said. 'If I don't have a description on my ticket, how can I be sure you'll give me back the coat and not something else when I return?'

'It goes in the books.'

'But all I've got is a number. So actually you could hand me any old thing you wanted, isn't that so?'

'Do you want a description or don't you?' the man asked.

'No,' she said. 'I trust you.'

The man wrote 'fifty dollars' opposite the word VALUE on both sections of the ticket, then he tore it in half along the perforations and slid the lower portion across the counter. He took a wallet from the inside pocket of his jacket and extracted five ten-dollar bills. 'The interest is three per cent a month,' he said.

'Yes, all right. And thank you. You'll take good care of it, won't you?'

The man nodded but said nothing.

'Shall I put it back in the box for you?'

'No,' the man said.

Mrs Bixby turned and went out of the shop on to the street where the taxi was waiting. Ten minutes later, she was home.

'Darling,' she said as she bent over and kissed her husband. 'Did you miss me?'

Cyril Bixby laid down the evening paper and glanced at the watch on his wrist. 'It's twelve and a half minutes past six,' he said. 'You're a bit late, aren't you?'

'I know. It's those dreadful trains. Aunt Maude sent you her love as usual. I'm dying for a drink, aren't you?'

The husband folded his newspaper into a neat rectangle and placed it on the arm of his chair. Then he stood up and crossed over to the sideboard. His wife remained in the centre of the room pulling off her gloves, watching him carefully, wondering how long she ought to wait. He had his back to her now, bending forward to measure the gin, putting his face right up close to the measurer and peering into it as though it were a patient's mouth.

It was funny how small he always looked after the Colonel. The Colonel was huge and bristly, and when you were near to him he smelled faintly of horseradish. This one was small and neat and bony and he didn't really smell of anything at all, except peppermint drops, which he sucked to keep his breath nice for the patients.

'See what I've bought for measuring the vermouth,' he said, holding up a calibrated glass beaker. 'I can get it to the nearest milligram with this.'

'Darling, how clever.'

I really must try to make him change the way he dresses, she told herself. His suits are just too ridiculous for words. There had been a time when she thought they were wonderful, those Edwardian jackets with high lapels and six buttons down the front, but now they merely seemed absurd. So did the narrow stovepipe trousers. You had to have a special sort of face to wear things like that, and Cyril just didn't have it. His was a long bony countenance with a narrow nose and a slightly **prognathous**

---

prognathous projecting

jaw, and when you saw it coming up out of the top of one of those tightly fitting old-fashioned suits it looked like a caricature of Sam Weller. He probably thought it looked like Beau Brummel. It was a fact that in the office he invariably greeted female patients with his white coat unbuttoned so that they would catch a glimpse of the trappings underneath; and in some obscure way this was obviously meant to convey the impression that he was a bit of a dog. But Mrs Bixby knew better. The plumage was a bluff. It meant nothing. It reminded her of an ageing peacock strutting on the lawn with only half its feathers left. Or one of those fatuous self-fertilizing flowers – like the dandelion. A dandelion never has to get fertilized for the setting of its seed, and all those brilliant yellow petals are just a waste of time, a boast, a masquerade. What's the word biologists use? Subsexual. A dandelion is subsexual. So, for that matter, are the summer broods of water fleas. It sounds a bit like Lewis Carroll, she thought – water fleas and dandelions and dentists.

'Thank you, darling,' she said, taking the Martini and seating herself on the sofa with her handbag on her lap. 'And what did *you* do last night?'

'I stayed on in the office and cast a few inlays. I also got my accounts up to date.'

'Now really, Cyril, I think it's high time you let other people do your donkey work for you. You're much too important for that sort of thing. Why don't you give the inlays to the mechanic?'

'I prefer to do them myself. I'm extremely proud of my inlays.'

'I know you are, darling, and I think they're absolutely wonderful. They're the best inlays in the whole world. But I don't want you to burn yourself out. And why doesn't that Pulteney woman do the accounts? That's part of her job, isn't it?'

'She does do them. But I have to price everything up first. She doesn't know who's rich and who isn't.'

'This Martini is perfect,' Mrs Bixby said, setting down her glass on the side table. 'Quite perfect.' She opened her bag and took out a handkerchief as if to blow her nose. 'Oh look!' she cried, seeing the ticket. 'I forgot to show you this! I found it just now on the seat of my taxi. It's got a number on it, and I thought it might be a lottery ticket or something, so I kept it.'

She handed the small piece of stiff brown paper to her husband, who took it in his fingers and began examining it minutely from all angles, as though it were a suspect tooth.

'You know what this is?' he said slowly.

'No dear, I don't.'

'It's a pawn ticket.'

'A what?'

'A ticket from a pawnbroker. Here's the name and address of the shop – somewhere on Sixth Avenue.'

'Oh dear, I *am* disappointed. I was hoping it might be a ticket for the Irish Sweep.'

'There's no reason to be disappointed,' Cyril Bixby said. 'As a matter of fact this could be rather amusing.'

'Why could it be amusing, darling?'

He began explaining to her exactly how a pawn ticket worked, with particular reference to the fact that anyone possessing the ticket was entitled to claim the article. She listened patiently until he had finished his lecture.

'You think it's worth claiming?' she asked.

'I think it's worth finding out what it is. You see this figure of fifty dollars that's written here? You know what that means?'

'No, dear, what does it mean?'

'It means that the item in question is almost certain to be something quite valuable.'

'You mean it'll be worth fifty dollars?'

'More like five hundred.'

'Five hundred!'

'Don't you understand?' he said. 'A pawnbroker never gives you more than about a tenth of the real value.'

'Good gracious! I never knew that.'

'There's a lot of things you don't know, my dear. Now you listen to me. Seeing that there's no name and address of the owner . . .'

'But surely there's something to say who it belongs to?'

'Not a thing. People often do that. They don't want anyone to know they've been to a pawnbroker. They're ashamed of it.'

'Than you think we can keep it?'

'Of course we can keep it. This is now *our* ticket.'

'You mean *my* ticket,' Mrs Bixby said firmly. 'I found it.'

'My dear girl, what *does* it matter? The important thing is that we are now in a position to go and redeem it any time we like for only fifty dollars. How about that?'

'Oh, what fun!' she cried. 'I think it's terribly exciting, especially when we don't even know what it is. It could be *anything*, isn't that right, Cyril? Absolutely anything!'

'It could indeed, although it's most likely to be either a ring or a watch.'

'But wouldn't it be marvellous if it was *a real* treasure? I mean something *really* old, like a wonderful old vase or a Roman statue.'

'There's no knowing what it might be, my dear. We shall just have to wait and see.'

'I think it's absolutely fascinating! Give me the ticket and I'll rush over first thing Monday morning and find out!'

'I think I'd better do that.'

'Oh no!' she cried. 'Let *me* do it!'

'I think not. I'll pick it up on my way to work.'

'But it's *my* ticket! *Please* let me do it, Cyril! Why should *you* have all the fun?'

'You don't know these pawnbrokers, my dear. You're liable to get cheated.'

'I wouldn't get cheated, honestly I wouldn't. Give the ticket to me, please!'

'Also you have to have fifty dollars,' he said, smiling. 'You have to pay out fifty dollars in cash before they'll give it to you.'

'I've got that,' she said. 'I think.'

'I'd rather you didn't handle it, if you don't mind.'

'But Cyril, I *found* it. It's mine. Whatever it is, it's mine, isn't that right?'

'Of course it's yours, my dear. There's no need to get so worked up about it.'

'I'm not. I'm just excited, that's all.'

'I suppose it hasn't occurred to you that this might be something entirely masculine – a pocket-watch, for example, or a set of shirt-studs. It isn't only women that go to pawnbrokers, you know.'

'In that case I'll give it to you for Christmas,' Mrs Bixby said magnanimously. 'I'll be delighted. But if it's a woman's thing, I want it myself. Is that agreed?'

'That sounds very fair. Why don't you come with me when I collect it?'

Mrs Bixby was about to say yes to this, but caught herself just in time. She had no wish to be greeted like an old customer by the pawnbroker in her husband's presence.

'No,' she said slowly. 'I don't think I will. You see, it'll be even more thrilling if I stay behind and wait. Oh, I do hope it isn't going to be something that neither of us wants.'

'You've got a point there,' he said. 'If I don't think it's worth fifty dollars, I won't even take it.'

'But you said it would be worth five hundred.'

'I'm quite sure it will. Don't worry.'

'Oh, Cyril. I can hardly wait! Isn't it exciting?'

'It's amusing,' he said, slipping the ticket into his waistcoat pocket. 'There's no doubt about that.'

Monday morning came at last, and after breakfast Mrs Bixby followed her husband to the door and helped him on with his coat.

'Don't work too hard, darling,' she said.

'No, all right.'

'Home at six?'

'I hope so.'

'Are you going to have time to go to that pawnbroker?' she asked.

'My God, I forgot all about it. I'll take a cab and go there now. It's on my way.'

'You haven't lost the ticket, have you?'

'I hope not,' he said, feeling in his waistcoat pocket. 'No, here it is.'

'And you have enough money?'

'Just about.'

'Darling,' she said, standing close to him and straightening his tie, which was perfectly straight. 'If it happens to be something nice, something you think I might like, will you telephone me as soon as you get to the office?'

'If you want me to, yes.'

'You know, I'm sort of hoping it'll be something for you, Cyril. I'd much rather it was for you than for me.'

'That's very generous of you, my dear. Now I must run.'

About an hour later, when the telephone rang, Mrs Bixby was across the room so fast she had the receiver off the hook before the first ring had finished.

'I got it!' he said.

'You did! Oh, Cyril, what was it? Was it something good?'

'Good!' he cried. 'It's fantastic! You wait till you get your eyes on this! You'll swoon!'

'Darling, what is it? Tell me quick!'

'You're a lucky girl, that's what you are.'

'It's for me, then?'

'Of course it's for you. Though how in the world it ever got to be pawned for only fifty dollars I'll be damned if I know. Someone's crazy.'

'Cyril! Stop keeping me in suspense! I can't bear it!'

'You'll go mad when you see it.'

'What is it?'

'Try to guess.'

Mrs Bixby paused. Be careful, she told herself. Be very careful now.

'A necklace,' she said.

'Wrong.'

'A diamond ring.'

'You're not even warm. I'll give you a hint. It's something you can wear.'

'Something I can wear? You mean like a hat?'

'No, it's not a hat,' he said, laughing.

'For goodness' sake, Cyril! Why don't you tell me?'

'Because I want it to be a surprise. I'll bring it home with me this evening.'

'You'll do nothing of the sort!' she cried. 'I'm coming right down there to get it now!'

'I'd rather you didn't do that.'

'Don't be silly, darling. Why shouldn't I come?'

'Because I'm too busy. You'll disorganize my whole morning schedule. I'm half an hour behind already.'

'Then I'll come in the lunch hour. All right?'

'I'm not having a lunch hour. Oh well, come at one-thirty then, while I'm having a sandwich. Goodbye.'

At half past one precisely, Mrs Bixby arrived at Mr Bixby's place of business and rang the bell. Her husband, in his white dentist's coat, opened the door himself.

'Oh, Cyril, I'm so excited!'

'So you should be. You're a lucky girl, did you know that?' He led her down the passage and into the surgery.

'Go and have your lunch, Miss Pulteney,' he said to the assistant, who was busy putting instruments into the sterilizer. 'You can finish that when you come back.' He waited until the girl had gone, then he walked over to a closet that he used for hanging up his clothes and stood in front of it, pointing with his finger. 'It's in there, he said. 'Now – shut your eyes.'

Mrs Bixby did as she was told. Then she took a deep breath and held it, and in the silence that followed she could hear him opening the cupboard door and there was a soft swishing sound as he pulled out a garment from among the other things hanging there.

'All right! You can look!'

'I don't dare to,' she said, laughing.

'Go on. Take a peek.'

Coyly, beginning to giggle, she raised one eyelid a fraction of an inch, just enough to give her a dark blurry view of the man standing there in his white overalls holding something up in the air.

'Mink!' he cried. 'Real mink!'

At the sound of the magic word she opened her eyes quick, and at the same time she actually started forward in order to clasp the coat in her arms.

But there was no coat. There was only a ridiculous little fur neckpiece dangling from her husband's hand.

'Feast your eyes on that!' he said, waving it in front of her face.

Mrs Bixby put a hand up to her mouth and started backing away. I'm going to scream, she told herself. I just know it. I'm going to scream.

'What's the matter, my dear? Don't you like it?' He stopped waving the fur and stood staring at her, waiting for her to say something.

'Why yes,' she stammered. 'I…I…think it's…it's lovely… really lovely.'

'Quite took your breath away for a moment there, didn't it?'

'Yes, it did.'

'Magnificent quality,' he said. 'Fine colour, too. You know something, my dear? I reckon a piece like this would cost you two or three hundred dollars at least if you had to buy it in a shop.'

'I don't doubt it.'

There were two skins, two narrow mangy-looking skins with their heads still on them and glass beads in their eye sockets and little paws hanging down. One of them had the rear end of the other in its mouth, biting it.

'Here,' he said. 'Try it on.' He leaned forward and draped the thing round her neck, then stepped back to admire. 'It's perfect. It really suits you. It isn't everyone who has mink, my dear.'

'No, it isn't.'

'Better leave it behind when you go shopping or they'll all think we're millionaires and start charging us double.'

'I'll try to remember that, Cyril.'

'I'm afraid you mustn't expect anything else for Christmas. Fifty dollars was rather more than I was going to spend anyway.'

He turned away and went over to the basin and began washing his hands. 'Run along now, my dear, and buy yourself a nice lunch. I'd take you out myself but I've got old man Gorman in the waiting-room with a broken clasp on his denture.'

Mrs Bixby moved towards the door.

I'm going to kill that pawnbroker, she told herself. I'm going right back there to the shop this very minute and I'm going to throw this filthy neckpiece right in his face and if he refuses to give me back my coat I'm going to kill him.

'Did I tell you I was going to be late home tonight?' Cyril Bixby said, still washing his hands.

'No.'

'It'll probably be at least eight-thirty the way things look at the moment. It may even be nine.'

'Yes, all right. Good-bye.' Mrs Bixby went out, slamming the door behind her.

At that precise moment, Miss Pulteney, the secretary-assistant, came sailing past her down the corridor on her way to lunch.

'Isn't it a gorgeous day?' Miss Pulteney said as she went by, flashing a smile. There was a lilt in her walk, a little whiff of perfume attending her, and she looked like a queen, just exactly like a queen in the beautiful black mink coat that the Colonel had given to Mrs Bixby.

A Place on the Piano
Eva Ibbotson

Introduction

I was born in Vienna many years ago and when I was a small girl Hitler began rounding up all the people he didn't care for – Jews and gypsies and democrats – and sending them to camps where most of them died.

My own family and close friends all escaped and made happy new lives in Britain but I had a small cousin called Marianne, aged seven, who vanished with her family and was never heard of again.

She must, I suppose, have perished along with millions of others, but I have never quite stopped wondering about her, and sometimes I've imagined that somehow, somewhere, she was still alive. It seemed so terrible that I, who was the same age, should find safety in my new country and that she should disappear into darkness. And because I'm a writer I have thought of many ways in which her story could after all have turned out to have a different ending.

'A Place on the Piano' is one such story – the events I have described did happen – mothers did save their babies by throwing them out of trains ... and perhaps, who knows, my little cousin Marianne was one such child, and lived.

A Place on the Piano

I always thought the war would end suddenly but it didn't – it sort of dribbled away. Six months after I stood with the other boys in my class outside Buckingham Palace – yelling for the king and queen because we'd defeated Hitler – the barrage balloons still floated like great silver grandfathers over the roofs of London. The park railings were still missing, St Paul's cathedral stood in a sea of rubble and there was nothing to be bought in the shops.

My teacher had explained it to me. 'Wars are expensive, Michael,' he said. 'They have to be paid for.'

Rationing got tighter – you still had to have coupons for clothes and fuel. Worst of all was the food. You could hardly see the meat ration with the naked eye, and some really weird things were issued by the government for us to eat. Tinned snoek, for example. Snoek is a South African fish and when Cook opened the tin it turned out to be a bluish animal with terrifying spikes, swimming in a sea of gelatinous goo – and the smell was unspeakable.

'This time they've gone too far,' she said, and she tried to give it to the cat, who sneered and turned away.

I knew quite a lot about rationing because I was a sort of kitchen boy. Not that I worked in the kitchen exactly; I'd just won a scholarship to the grammar school, but I lived below stairs in the basement of a large house belonging to a family called Glossop, where my mother was the housekeeper. We'd lived there, in London, all through the war.

I remember the snoek particularly because we were just wondering what to do with it when the bell went and my mother was called upstairs.

When she came back she looked really happy and excited. 'Little Marianne Gerstenberger has been found. She's alive!'

It was incredible news. Marianne had been thrown out of a cattle train when she was a baby. It was her own mother who had done it. She'd been rounded up with some other Jews and she was on her way to a concentration camp when she found a weak place in one of the boards behind the latrine. She got the others to help her work on it to make a small hole. And then she bundled up the baby, and when the train stopped for a moment she managed to push her out on to the track.

We'd heard a lot about bravery during the last six years of war: soldiers in Burma stumbling on, dying of thirst; parachutists at Arnheim, and of course the Spitfire pilots who had saved us in the Blitz. But the story of Marianne caught us all.

'To do that,' said my mother, 'to push your own baby out on to the track because you knew you were going to your death…'

At first my mother had tried not to speak of what had happened when Hitler went mad and tried to exterminate the Jews. But my school was the kind where they told you things, and I'd seen the newsreels. I'd seen the bodies piled up when the Allies opened up the camps, and the skeletons which were supposed to be people. Marianne's parents had both perished, but now, as the news came through from the Red Cross in Switzerland, it seemed that the baby had survived. She had been found by a peasant family who had taken her in and was living in East Germany, close to the border with Poland.

'They're going to fetch her,' said my mother. 'They're going to take her in.' And there were tears in her eyes.

'They' were her employers – the Glossops – who lived in the house above us and who she served. The Glossops were not Jewish, but Marianne's mother had been married to the son of their Jewish business partners in Berlin. Glossop and Gerstenberger had been a well-known firm of exporters.

'They're going to adopt her,' my mother went on. She didn't often speak warmly about the Glossops, but I could hear the admiration in her voice.

'She'll live like a little princess,' said Cook. 'Imagine, after being brought up with peasants.'

Everyone agreed with this: the kids in my school, the people in the shops, the tradesmen who came to deliver goods to the basement. Because the Glossops, weren't just well off, they were properly rich. Their house was the largest in the square, double-fronted – and furnished as though the war had never been. To go up the service stairs and through the green baize door into the house was like stepping into a different world.

Mrs Glossop and her mother-in-law had spent the war in a hotel in the Lake District to get away from the bombs; and her daughter, Daphne, who was ten years old, had been away at boarding school, but the house had stayed open because Mr Glossop used it when he was in town on business, which meant that the servants had to keep it ready for him whenever he wanted.

So my mother and I went upstairs most days to check the blackout curtains and make sure the shutters were closed and none of the window panes had cracked in the raids – and I knew the house as well as I knew the dark rooms in the basement where we lived, along with the cook and old Tom, the chauffeur-handyman.

I knew the dining room with its heavy button-backed chairs and the carved sideboard where they kept the napkin rings and the cruets which Tom polished every week. I knew the drawing room with its thick Turkish carpet and massive sofas – and I knew old Mrs Glossop's boudoir on the first floor with the gilt mirrors and claw-footed tables – and the piano.

I knew the piano very well. I remember once when I was upstairs helping my mother I heard a V1 rocket cut out above me, which meant I had about half a minute before it came down and exploded – and without thinking I dived under the piano.

It was an enormous piano – a Steinway Concert Grand – but I'd never heard anybody play it. It was a piano for keeping relations on. On the dark red chenille cover which protected it were rows of Glossops in silver frames: old Glossops and young ones,

Glossops on their horses and Glossops in their university gowns. There were Glossop children in their school uniforms or holding cricket bats, and there were Glossop women in their presentation dresses ready to go to court. There was even a Glossop who had been knighted, and as I lay there, waiting for the bomb to fall, I wasn't in the least bit scared – I didn't feel anyone would dare to destroy a whole army of Glossops, and I was right. The rocket came down three streets away.

And now Marianne Gerstenberger, who was just seven years old, would have her own place on the piano, and be a Glossop too.

The preparations for Marianne began straight away, and we all threw ourselves into the work. It may sound silly, but I think it was then that we realized that the war was well and truly over, and that good things were happening in the world.

'We'll put her in the room next to Daphne's,' said Mrs Glossop – and she gave my mother a list of all the things that needed to be done. New curtains of pale blue satin to be sewn, and the bed canopied with the same material. A white fur rug on the floor, the walls repapered with a design of forget-me-nots and rosebuds, and a new dressing table to be lined with a matching pattern. Furniture was difficult to get – you had to have coupons for nearly everything – but when you own three department stores the rules don't really apply. The Glossops had always had everything they wanted, and that included food. Parcels from America had come all through the war and they were coming still.

'She can have my dolls – I don't play with them any more,' said Daphne, but Mrs Glossop ordered a whole batch of new dolls and fluffy toys and games from the store.

'Of course she'll be a little savage,' said old Mrs Glossop. 'We must be patient with her.'

She sent my mother out to get one of the napkin rings engraved with Marianne's name and I imagined the little girl sitting in the big solemn dining room with all the Glossop ancestors looking down from the wall, carefully rolling up her damask napkin after every meal.

Actually I knew exactly the sort of life Marianne was going to lead, because of Daphne.

Daphne didn't speak to me much; she was not the sort of girl who spoke to servants. A year earlier I'd pulled off an Alsatian who was holding her at bay as she played in the gardens of the square, and got quite badly bitten, and while my hands were bandaged she was positively friendly, but it didn't last.

Mostly Daphne was away at boarding school, but when she was at home she led a very busy life. On Saturday morning she put on her jodhpurs and Tom drove her to the park where she went riding – trotting down the sanded paths and greeting other children on well-groomed ponies. On Monday afternoon, she carried her dancing shoes in a velvet bag to Miss Bigelow's Academy and learned ballet, and on Thursdays she did elocution with a lady called Madame Farnari.

Marianne would do all this – but not for long, because as soon as she had her eighth birthday she would be taken to a school outfitter to buy a brown velour hat and a brown gymslip and a hockey stick and go off with Daphne to St Hilda's, where the school motto was 'Play straight and play the game'.

'When you think what that school costs, and the kind of children who go there – all those honourables and what have you – it'll be a wonderful thing for the little thing,' said old Tom, the chauffeur. 'Mind you, she'll have a lot to learn.'

As it turned out, we had several months to get ready for Marianne, because even the Glossops didn't find it easy to get the passports and permits and papers that were needed to bring

Marianne to Britain. Things were made more difficult because the village where Marianne now lived was in the part of Germany that was occupied by the Russians and they were very strict about who could come into their zone and who could not.

But at last a permit came through, allowing two people to travel to Orthausen and pick up the little girl. The permit was for a particular week in July and now my mother was sent for again. What's more, she was asked to sit down, which was unusual.

'It's so awkward, such a nuisance,' said Mrs Glossop to my mother. 'But the permit covers the day of the royal garden party and I've been asked to attend. I simply couldn't miss that – and two days later it's Daphne's prize-giving at St Hilda's and of course I must go down for that.'

My mother waited, wondering why she had been summoned.

'My husband would go and fetch the little girl, but he has the annual meeting of the cricket club and then a very important Rotary dinner in Aberdeen at which he's been asked to speak.' She bent forward and fixed my mother with a stern eye. 'So I want you to fetch Marianne. It's so convenient because you speak German.'

This was true. My mother had been studying modern languages at university when my father had married and deserted her, all in three months.

But my mother said she couldn't leave me. This was nonsense, of course, but she said it very firmly. I think she felt that the Glossops should go themselves to fetch their new daughter – or perhaps she was nervous. Since my father betrayed her, she had looked for a quiet life – a life where the two of us would be safe.

'Well, the permit is for two people. I don't see why Michael shouldn't go with you; we don't have to say that he's only twelve years old.'

So it was my mother and I who went to fetch Marianne Gerstenberger, but before we left we were given some very important instructions.

'Marianne has a birthmark on her arm,' said Mrs Glossop. 'Her mother wrote to us about it when she was born. It's on her right arm and it runs from her shoulder to her elbow – and you must make absolutely sure that she does have that mark and in the right place. It's one thing to adopt the daughter of one's husband's partner and another to take in any stray that wants a comfortable home.' And she told us that though Marianne's name had been pinned to her blanket, it was possible that in those frightful times the baby's things had been stolen and given to some other child.

'We will make sure,' promised my mother – and two weeks later we set off.

It was quite a journey. Ordinary people hadn't been allowed to travel all through the war and of course I was excited, crossing the Channel, getting a train to go through the Netherlands and Germany.

Or rather, five trains. Most of the rolling stock had been destroyed in Allied bombing raids. We stopped and started and were pushed out on to the platform and back in again. There was no food to be had on the train, or water, and I couldn't help wondering if it was because she knew how uncomfortable the journey was going to be that Mrs Glossop had decided to send my mother instead. We went though towns that were nothing but heaps of rubble and countryside with burnt and empty fields. It was odd to think that it was we who had caused all this destruction. I'd thought of bombing as something that the Germans did.

We spent the night in a cold and gloomy little hotel on the Belgian border, and the next day we travelled east through Germany.

I asked my mother if this was the route that Marianne's mother would have travelled on her last journey but she didn't know.

We were going through farmland now: fields and copses and little villages. The houses looked poor and small but there were a few animals: cows and sheep. The peasants were struggling to get back to a normal life.

We had to change twice more on to branch lines, travelling on trains so old that we didn't think they would manage to pull their loads. Then in the late afternoon we reached Orthausen.

The village that Marianne lived in was not directly on the railway. The woman who found her must have carried her bundle a long way to her house. My mother and I now walked that road, trudging along the white dust village street with our bags and turning off along a track which ran beside a stream.

Then, late in the afternoon, we crossed a small bridge and came to a wooden house standing by itself in a clearing.

Marianne was sitting on the steps of the porch. She was holding a tortoiseshell kitten on her lap and talking to it – not fussing over it, just telling it to behave. She spoke in German, but I knew exactly what she was saying.

She had thick, fawn, curly hair and brown eyes and she wore a **dirndl**, and over it a knitted jersey which covered her arms. When she saw us she put down the kitten and then she reached for the bag my mother carried and led us into the house.

The woman who had found Marianne on the railway track was called Mrs Wasilewski. She was very pale with a screwed-down bun of fair hair and a tight mouth. To me she looked like a death's head, so white and forbidding, and I was glad that we were going to take Marianne away from such a cold, stern

---

dirndl a dress with a full skirt

woman. But Marianne went up to her trustingly and said, here were the visitors from England, and I realized that she did not yet know why we had come.

Mrs Wasilewski offered us some **ersatz** coffee and slices of dark bread spread with dripping. Her husband was away, working in a sawmill in the north of the country for the summer, to earn some extra money. When we had eaten, Marianne turned to me and took me by the hand, and said, '*Komm,*' and I got up and followed her.

When somebody takes you by the hand and says '*Komm*', it is not difficult to guess what they are saying, but it still seems odd to me that from the first moment I understood Marianne so completely, and that she understood me.

The Wasilewskis had a smallholding, but the Germans had commandeered the horse at the beginning of the war and the Russians had taken the cow at the end of it. All the same, the animals that were left seemed to satisfy Marianne. She introduced me to the two goats – a white one, called Bella, and a bad-tempered brown one, called Sidonia, after a disagreeable lady who scowled at everybody in the church. She showed me the five hens and told me their names and the rabbits and the new piglet, honking in the straw.

Actually, it was more than showing – she sort of presented them to me, giving me the animals to hold as if hanging on to a squawking chicken or a lop-eared rabbit must make me the happiest person in the world.

It was far too late to try and make our way back that night – no one knew how the trains would run. Mrs Wasilewski – still unsmiling and gaunt – led us to a loft with two goose-down duvets on a slatted wooden board and we went to bed.

---

ersatz substitute (real coffee was hard to obtain)

I was sure we'd leave the next morning, but we didn't. My mother helped Mrs Wasilewski with the housework and once again Marianne put out her hand and said, '*Komm*,' and once again I came.

She led me to a part of the stream where the water ran clear over a bed of pebbles. Both of us took off our shoes, but she kept on her jersey, and we walked along the river bed, dredging up bright and glittering stones.

'*Nicht Gold*,' she said, holding out a yellow-veined stone and shaking her head, but she was smiling. She didn't want gold, I could see that. She wanted brightness.

The stream was full of sticklebacks and newts and tiny frogs; all the creatures too small to have been stolen or pillaged in war.

After a while a boy and a girl appeared – a brother and sister – and Marianne introduced me, carefully pronouncing my name in the English way I'd taught her.

We came to a bridge where the current ran quite fast and we each chose a stick and raced it from one side to the other. I hadn't done that since I was at infant school, but you can't go wrong with Pooh sticks, and I found myself wondering if they played it at St Hilda's.

Mrs Wasilewski, still grim and silent, gave us lunch – pieces of salt bacon with beetroot and cabbage from her garden – and afterwards Marianne took me out and showed me the rows of vegetables, and picked a pea pod from the vine and opened it, dropping the shelled peas into my palm.

All that day Marianne stretched out her hand and said, '*Komm*.' She showed me a hedgehog asleep in the potting shed and a place where raspberries grew wild, and I made her a whistle out of a hazel twig. I'd brought my Swiss Army knife, and the whistle was a good one. They don't always work but this one did.

Even the next day my mother said nothing about leaving. We slept on the floor; the work she was helping with was far harder than any that she did in England and Mrs Wasilewski still went round like a zombie, but my mother didn't seem in any hurry to return.

That day Marianne showed me her special tree. It was an ancient oak standing on its own on a small hill and it was the kind of tree that is a whole world in itself. There were hollows in the trunk where squirrels had stored their nuts; beetles sheltered under the bark and a woodpecker tapped in the branches.

Marianne had not *built* a tree-house because the tree *was* her house. She explained this as we climbed up – and that it was in this house that she kept her treasures. They lived in a tin with a picture of cough lozenges on the lid, and she showed them to me, one by one. There was a tortoiseshell hair slide, a little bent; a bracelet made out of glass beads; a propelling pencil – and her most important possession: a small bear, carved roughly out of wood, which Mr Wasilewski had made on her last birthday. Then she took the whistle I had made for her out of her pocket and laid it carefully in the tin beside the other things, and closed the lid.

But the best thing about the tree was the view. Because it stood on a knoll you could see the surrounding countryside for miles. Marianne pointed to a small farm and told me that the man who had lived there had been killed on the Eastern Front. He'd been a German, of course – maybe a Nazi – but Marianne's face grew sad as she told me about him, which was strange because her mother's people had been so horribly persecuted by men like him.

If she was the child we thought she was...

But in the opposite direction was a low, red-roofed house and she told me that the man who owned it had a litter of sheepdog puppies and he was going to let her have one. There was enough food now to keep a dog, she said joyfully; it was no longer forbidden.

I didn't say anything. She would never be able to bring a dog into England; the quarantine regulations were far too strict, and the Glossops said it wasn't fair to keep animals in town. Even the cat we kept in the basement knew better than to make her way upstairs.

Then on the morning of the third day my mother called me into the kitchen. Mrs Wasilewski was there, more silent and morose than ever. There was a bundle on the table: the blanket Marianne had been wrapped in, I guessed, when she was found on the track, and a few baby clothes. Mrs Wasilewski called Marianne to her side and she came. For the first time, she looked puzzled and anxious.

'Wait,' said my mother. 'We must make sure we have the right child.' And very gently she said, 'Will you take your jersey off, Marianne, and your blouse?'

Marianne looked at Mrs Wasilewski, who nodded. Then she took off her jersey and undid the drawstring of her blouse.

Now she stood before us with both arms bare. From her shoulder to her elbow, her right arm was covered in a dark brown birthmark.

It was exactly what the Glossops had described to us. Without a doubt, the child who stood before us was the child who had been thrown from the train.

My mother and I looked at each other. Mrs Wasilewski stood like a ramrod, her mouth tight shut. Marianne, still puzzled, reached for her blouse and began to put it on.

The room was very still. Then my mother cleared her throat and looked at me again. She looked at me hard.

'What a pity,' she said clearly to Mrs Wasilewski. 'I'm so sorry. I'm afraid this is the wrong child. We can't take her back with us – her birthmark is on the wrong arm.' And then, softly: 'She will have to stay with you.'

The silence was broken suddenly by a gasp – followed by a kind of juddering sound. Then Mrs Wasilewski went mad. Her head dropped forward on to the table and she began to cry – but you can't call it crying. She erupted in tears, she became completely drenched in them, her hair came down and fell in damp strands across the table. I have never in all my life heard anybody cry like that.

When she lifted her head again she was a totally different woman; she was rosy, she laughed, she hugged my mother and me. And I understood at once – that this woman who had made Marianne's world with such loving care had been almost destroyed at the thought of losing her.

In the train my mother said, 'I think we'll just say there was no birthmark. We don't want any further fuss about left or right.'

'Yes.' The train chugged on through what had once been enemy territory and was now just the great plain of central Europe. 'I'm going back,' I said. 'Later.' And then: 'Not much later.'

'Yes, I know,' said my mother. 'And I'm going on.'

(And she did too. She gave up her job with the Glossops and went back to finish her degree. We lived in two small rooms and were very happy.)

When we got back we were called up to the boudoir so that the old lady too could hear our story.

'Oh, well,' said Mrs Glossop, when we'd finished. 'It's a pity, when we had so much to offer a child. But it doesn't sound as though she would have fitted in.'

And my mother looked at the piano, with its two dozen important Glossops in silver frames, and said no, she wouldn't have fitted in. She wouldn't have fitted in at all.

The Daughter
Jacqueline Wilson

I turn the handle of the spit. Turn and turn and turn. The fat from the fowl spatters my face. The great fire scorches me until I am half-cooked myself.

I turn and turn and turn though my back is breaking, turn though my hands are blistered. My mouth is so dry I can barely swallow but I finished my mug of small beer an hour ago. I am so weary that my eyes start closing, c-l-o-s-i-n-g...

'Keep turning, you useless feeble girl!' roars the Master Meat Cook.

The other scullions snigger.

The Cook is kind to the boys. He gives them the choicest leftovers and when they've done their chores he joins them in their games of football in the gardens.

The Cook throws the blown-up pig's bladder at my head, knocking me smartly so that my eyes sting.

'There! That will wake you up,' says the Cook.

He hates me. He hates me even though I am his daughter, his only child. He hates me *because* I am his daughter, his only child. He hates me because I killed my mother.

She was the Sweetmeat Cook. When my father speaks of her he savours her name as if her own rosewater candies were melting on his tongue. They were brought up together in the Palace kitchens, childhood sweethearts. They wed when they came of age and were delighted when my mother grew big with child. A lusty boy to follow in his father's footsteps in the Palace.

But I was a girl, a red-faced bawling babe who nearly tore my mother apart. She took me in her arms at last and I stared at her with my great green eyes.

'Witch's eyes,' says my father, spitting. 'You looked at your mother and put a curse on her. She died of a fever three days after.'

He's never said it, but I know he wishes I'd died too. But he paid for me to be brought up in the village, and when I was six he took me to live with him inside the Palace. Not as his child. As the junior scullion. To scrub and scrape and steep – and to turn and turn and turn the spit for the roasting meat. Boar and beef, capons, pheasants, quails and swans.

When Father thwacks the sides of meat with his axe his face is contorted and I jump at each thud. When he skewers each limp bird body I tremble. When he chops off a head I shut my eyes tight.

I have to scurry round and sweep up the eyes and beaks, the paws and claws, the reeking ribbons of innards. Once I saved two severed swan's wings and tried to work out how to fix them to my back so I could fly far away. The wings withered and started to smell and I had to throw them on to the rubbish heap. I tried straddling the kitchen broom but my feet stayed flat on the floor. My father thinks me a witch but I see no evidence of any magic powers, black or white.

I pretend though. It's the only way I can stop the other scullions making my life even more of a misery. When their pokes and prods become too vicious I raise my head and stare straight at them, widening my eyes until they water.

'Lizzie's giving us the witch's eyes!' they say, giggling nervously. 'Foolish girl! Can't scare us.'

But they back away, ducking their heads, out of my line of sight. I scare them all right.

I once tried the eye trick on Father, when I caught him in the corner with the Pudding Cook, the woman who was once my poor dead mother's friend. I thought of Mother underneath the cold earth, eternally unembraced. I widened my eyes – and Father saw me over her shoulder.

He hit me then. He beat me until neither of my witch's eyes could open and for days the kitchen was a blur.

Turn and turn and turn. The spit is chock-a-block with flesh and fowl and there's still a vast heap of dead creatures waiting in the wet room. We are preparing for a huge celebratory banquet. The new Queen has withdrawn to her chambers and started her labours at dawn today. We are all awaiting the birth of the little Prince.

In the cool at the far end of the kitchen the Sugar Cook has fashioned a sugar cradle that really rocks and now he is modelling a **marchpane** babe, its head eerily real, its arms and legs neatly tucked up, its bare bottom on show for all to gawp at.

'And if it's a girl they can always pull off its twiddly bit,' one of the scullions giggles.

The Sauce Cook hits him with her ladle and my father frowns. It is not a laughing matter. The King has to have a son and heir. That is why he discarded the first Queen and little Princess. Now he has the new Queen, the one they whisper is also a witch. She has certainly bewitched the King, but so long as she gives birth to a fine healthy son she will need no magic charms.

It will be a son. The finest astrologers in the land have consulted their charts and declared it to the King. The Royal Physicians have prodded the Queen beneath her farthingale and agreed that the unborn infant is definitely a male child. The Queen's Ladies have performed all the usual tests and tricks and each and every time they are united in their testimony: a boy.

The Palace is agog with the good news – but as the hours progress there is a growing tension. The Queen's chambers are at the other end of the Palace, but every now and then I fancy I can hear her high-pitched screams.

---

marchpane marzipan

I turn and turn and turn, the fire slow and smouldering for the swan and turkey, but banked up to roaring heat to crisp the pork and sear the game birds.

As the hours pass the tensions worsen in the kitchen. Every table is covered with cooked meats, glistening gold and ruby red and rich brown – but maybe this is a banquet that will never be touched.

The new Queen has been in hard labour for too long. The Pudding Cook scurries the corridors and whispers with her friends in the bed chambers. She tells us that they've sent for the local Wise Woman.

'But she's a witch, everyone knows that!' my father gasps.

'A witch to help a witch,' says the Pudding Cook. 'She knows a secret trick of speeding labour.'

The Wise Woman works her magic charms. Just after four the Pudding Cook comes speeding back down the corridors.

'The babe is born! Alive and well – and the Queen too, though exhausted.'

'The King has his son!' my father shouts, punching the air with his fist, and the kitchen rocks with hurrahs.

'No! No, it is a daughter, a girl!' says the Pudding Cook.

There's a sudden appalled silence.

My father stares at me, his old sorrow sharpening his face.

'Turn!' he shouts.

I turn and turn and turn, eyes lowered, because I do not want another beating.

I roast the bird, though the banquet will be a sad affair. The Sweetmeat Cook mutilates his marchpane babe, decides it is too cruel a reminder, and starts to mix a vat of sugar and eggwhite, intent on wrapping the child with edible swaddling.

There's an order from the King! We are all allowed extra ale to drink the health of the Queen and her new child. Doubtless it would have been fine wine if a boy had been born. But the ale is welcome nonetheless, and the kitchen is soon a merry place for all but me. My father allows the scullions their share of ale too, but I am only permitted my usual small beer which fails to flush the cheeks or fuddle the brain.

My father is very flushed, very fuddled. He is fooling with the Pudding Cook, dipping his finger in syrup, writing sticky messages on her bare neck. But then word is sent from the Queen's chambers. Her Majesty is reviving and requires a good posset curd to build up her strength.

The Pudding Cook panics and gets to work with a great clattering of pans. She needs to seethe her milk on the fire so she elbows me out of the way. She starts cracking the eggs in her mixture, one after another, beating clumsily. Her face is red with effort, her hair hanging in her eyes. She fails to stir enough, and the fire is too fierce.

'It's curdling!' she wails. 'It's ruined!'

She turns to me. 'It's all your fault! You put the evil eye on it. You're a child of the Devil.'

She strikes at me with her spoon. I dodge, my arms flailing – and knock her whole bowl flying across the floor. She hits me again, knocking me over, so I roll into the fire, the fire, the fire...

My hands, my hands! But someone is soothing them with cool lotion and wrapping them in soft linen, singing to me gently all the while. Is it my mother? Have I died and gone to Heaven?

I open my eyes. I stare at two orbs as green as my own – but this is an old woman with wrinkles deep in her face and silver hair. She smiles at me, and I smile back in spite of the pain.

'Your daughter will recover,' she says over her shoulder.

'Thank you for your help, Wise Woman,' the Pudding Cook mumbles, chastened.

'I doubt her hands will heal though. She'll be good for nothing if she cannot turn that spit,' says my father. 'What use will the girl be then?'

'She would be of use to me. I have need of an apprentice,' says the Wise Woman. 'Pray let me take your daughter, Master Cook. I will give you a good price for her.'

She tips out half the purse of gold given to her by the Queen. My father does not argue. He stoops and gathers the coins before she can change her mind.

'You gave that vast sum for *me*!' I whisper, stunned, as she leads me away from the Palace on her old mare.

'Your father certainly does not hold you dear!'

'It is because I am evil. I killed my mother,' I confess. 'My father said that I stared at her with my green witch's eyes the day I was born and put a curse on her.'

'What nonsense,' says the Wise Woman, tucking her own shawl about my shoulders. 'All newborn babes have *blue* eyes. I of all women should know that.'

I can scarcely absorb this information.

'Even so,' I whisper, 'why should you waste a fortune on a useless girl-child?'

'Girls are of great value,' says the Wise Woman. 'We are entering a new age. The little red-haired babe born today will make a fine Queen of England.'

She wraps the shawl tight, like mock swaddling.

'And you shall be *my* babe, my little witch daughter – and one day you will be as wise a woman as me.'

The Princess Spy
Jamila Gavin

Introduction

Years ago, I picked up a book in an oriental bookshop called *Twenty Jakata Tales*, retold by Noor Inayat Khan. The stories were of the lives of the Buddha in his different animal reincarnations – nearly all about sacrifice. The blurb informed me that Noor Inayat Khan had been the war heroine, code-named 'Madeleine', who had been a secret agent during the Second World War and who was posthumously awarded the George Cross, the MBE and the Croix de Guerre Gold Star.

Posthumously. That word always had a strange ring to it: 'after death'. I vaguely wondered how she had died. Twenty years later, when I was asked to write a story about war, her name immediately leaped into my head. As I researched, I wondered why – if she had been such a heroine – was she so unknown, especially when she was a princess too? There were hints that she had been 'used' by powers in London to mislead the enemy, and it seems certain that she was betrayed by a French colleague. Now I found out why and how she died. She was shot by the Nazis as a spy.

Some knew her just for her beauty and **ephemeral** qualities, but others were convinced that it was only because she was so imbued in the Sufi philosophy she had learned from her father that she was able to find the courage and strength to sacrifice herself.

I also wanted to pay tribute to the thousands of Indians and other Commonwealth fighters and agents who gave their lives for the battle against fascism in the Second World War.

---

ephemeral short-lived

The Princess Spy
Code Name: Madeleine

Others think they know me
But I am mine; what I am, I am.

In the darkness I see no light. But there is a light in my soul which shines out and illumines my prison cell.

What can the tiger catch in the dark corners of his own lair?

In the darkness I hear no sound, but in my head I hear music, of course! Music.

Only sweet-voiced birds are imprisoned.

In my mouth I would taste only bitterness if I didn't have the memory of sweet almonds and lover's kisses.

They keep me chained to the wall like a savage dog, but I am a swallow, soaring, circling high on the air currents. Whatever they do to me, I will not let myself down. I have not betrayed my country, I have not betrayed my masters. I am a princess. The blood of the great Rajah, Tipoo Sultan, runs in my veins. I am of the warrior class. They can interrogate me all they want and torture me too, but I will not betray myself.

● ● ● ●

Her name was Noor.

Her father was an Indian prince, Hazrat Inayat Khan, a Muslim, a musician and a Sufi mystic. His reputation spread far and wide for his wise counselling – even as far as Moscow. There, the strange, powerful Russian Orthodox mystic monk, Rasputin, asked him to come to the Kremlin palace and bring his Sufi philosophy of peace and love to comfort the Tsar of All Russias, Tsar Nicholas, in his time of trouble. Russia was in turmoil. Nicholas didn't understand why. How could he, closed

73

away in his palaces, as far removed from his people as the sun is from the earth?

So, along with his young American wife, Nora, Hazrat arrived in Moscow. Their first child, Noor, was born in the Kremlin palace on 2 January 1914, when Europe was bristling with quarrels, intrigues and assassinations, leading up to the outbreak of the First World War that August. Russia, too, was seething with unrest and things were leading **inexorably** towards revolution.

The stone walls surround me, yet the chains fall from my limbs and I am an infant again, crawling up the long scarlet-carpeted staircase in the Russian palace. There is an outburst of girlish laughter, and a flurry of princesses surround me like swans, gathering me up, pinching my cheeks and passing me round like a parcel: Olga, Tatiana, Maria and Anastasia. 'Let me hold her! Let me!' Their voices tinkle like bells.

'Darling Alexis!' The princesses draw in their little brother – their precious boy who, one day, will be Tsar of All Russias. 'Here. Careful now, don't drop her!' and I am passed into the arms of a boy who looks at me with sad, solemn eyes.

Their eyes gleam at me through the years of darkness. 'They came for us,' they seem to say. 'Now they have come for you.'

Look! There I am again, bundled up in furs, crammed in among the Russian princesses on the back of a sleigh, pulled by jingling horses, flying across the flat, white, rigid landscape, and plunging into birch forests, their branches drooping with snow. 'Baba Yaga, the witch, is after us,' they whispered in my ear, making me shriek with joyful terror.

They are all dead now. The Tsar and his queen, my lovely swan princesses, all captured – not by Baba Yaga, but by the

---

inexorably unstoppably

Bolshevik revolutionaries, who shot them all those years ago; Alexis too – my little tsaravitch.

My father's face bends over me so tenderly. His beard is like a cloud and his dark eyes are deep pools of mystery. 'Go to sleep, my little hare,' he murmurs.

A hare? Am I the hare? Lord Buddha came as a hare, and was willing to allow himself to be eaten to feed a hungry person.

'Tell me another story,' she whimpers in the dark.

How she loved stories and made them tell her more, more, and when there were no more to tell, Noor made up her own.

Princess Noor was born to enchant. She was beautiful and talented. A child of the Muses – full of poetry, stories, dance and music. A child of rhythm – but a rhythm of her own – shy, soaring, circling among the ideas and philosophies that her father taught her.

How could her stiff English masters understand that?

When she stood before them – this dark, gleaming young woman who looked more suited to the bohemian cafes of Paris than the tight-lipped, English public school discipline of the War Office – they must have asked themselves, 'What on earth has she to offer?'

'Like the hare, my little princess, you can offer yourself.'

My father's voice counselled me in my head.

Oh, why did you have to die, dear father?

He is the only one I weep for. My torturers have made me scream and cry as they have tried in vain to make me talk, but those tears are different; they are because of my physical pain. The pain which makes me truly weep is deeper; it is the pain of betrayal and because I no longer know who is my friend and who my enemy. It is the pain of loss because you are dead and gone. Oh, Papa! We were all thrown into such agony when we heard of your death in India while we were so far away from you in Paris. Mama locked herself away in her room and would not come out. We couldn't bear to think that never again would we hear your music, never again hear your deep, silken voice and listen to your wise words. Yet now, in this empty silence, you speak to me. You are here after all, to give me courage.

'Death is just stepping into the light, dear daughter. Remember the hare? As he entered the fire to give his body so that others could eat, the fairy of light came and made the flames as cool as water.'

We are waves whose stillness is non-being.

It was 1940. The Nazis had overrun almost the whole of Europe and were now at the gates of Paris. 'We have to leave immediately,' Noor begged her mother, who had shunned the world for twelve years, leaving Noor to be the responsible one. 'We must get out now.' With great difficulty, she persuaded her mother to flee. They all joined a long train of refugees and headed for the coast, and managed to get on the last boat leaving for England. There, Noor and her brother wanted to help the war effort. He joined the Royal Air Force and she the Women's Auxiliary Air Force – the WAAF – and was assigned to its transport section. She was keen and dedicated. But surely she could do more?

Pinstripe-suited men discussed her, sitting on one side of a long, polished table. 'She asks to do more? We need more people in Paris. We could use her, perhaps.'

They summoned her before them.

Here in the darkness, Paris gleams out in my mind. Beautiful Paris. The boulevards are scattered with sunlight. I walk gaily, composing tunes in my head on my way to school, sniffing the honey-roasted peanuts they sell in the Luxembourg Gardens, as I cut through to St-Germain-des-Prés. I wriggle my fingers, remembering the exercises I have been practising. Paris is my home; it's where my friends are. It's where I feel alive and truly myself.

'If you send me to France, you are sending me home,' I told them.

● ● ● ●

'Let's see,' said Pinstripe, looking at the notes and files in front of him. 'You have been living in Paris with your mother, brother and sisters for the last seventeen years. Music student, writer of stories –' he glanced down at his notes – 'for children? You've broadcast on Paris radio – so your French is fluent – and you know the city well.'

'It's my home,' she repeated. 'I want to help.'

'Yes, well…' They conferred while she waited outside. 'Perhaps she would be of use,' said one.

'It will be dangerous,' said another with some compassion. 'If they catch her, she'll be shot.'

'It's war. Sacrifices have to be made.'

To the men of the War Office she looked so unsuited to this work – too otherworldly, too innocent, too much of a butterfly. Not British. Most were sceptical. After all, they had never sent in a woman radio operative before. What's more, she was an Indian. India was already in conflict with the British – trying to kick them out of India. Could they be sure that she could be trusted?

'If she can't be trusted,' a cold, dark voice spoke, 'all the better for playing a game with, my dear.'

The game. What game? Everyone knew there was a game, but so few knew who the players were and what the rules of the game were.

'Send her into France as one of our operatives. Give her a radio. Ask her to send and receive messages. We'll send her information – false information. She's sure to be caught and sure to be interrogated. At first, she won't speak, but – I know these sorts of people – she'll crack. She'll spill the beans. But they'll be our beans, and they'll swallow them whole.'

So she received her instructions. 'We want you to go to France. Meet up with the Resistance; be a radio operative. You will be given a transmitter and will learn the radio game,' they told her.

She was registered in her mother's name – Norah Baker – and her training began. For long weeks, she learned how to operate the radio, how to use the codes and ciphers they would give her. They told her about the Resistance cells all over France, full of people working to free France and the rest of Europe from the Nazis.

She would have to be flown in at night, landing in a field. She would have to connect with other agents and sympathizers, and be part of a group. She must learn how to collect information and radio it back to them, to live a double life. Her cover name was to be Jeanne-Marie Regnier, her code name, 'Madeleine'.

I am flying, flying! How beautiful. The darkness of my cell is illumined by the moon. I felt close to heaven, then, as we flew; and close to you, Papa, with the stars all around and the sea glistening below. How small I felt too. Infinitesimal. How could I make any difference?

Yes, daughter, you are but a drop of water in an illimitable sea, but each drop is there to make up the consciousness of the whole ocean.

The world looked marvellously tranquil in the cloudy moonshine that June night, when the Lysander took off from England. So peaceful. Impossible to think of the terrors and dangers that awaited her.

Suddenly, from far below, a shower of sparks from a fire sprayed upwards into the air like fireflies. 'That's them!' muttered the pilot, and the little plane circled and dropped lower and lower. It hadn't seemed real till then. Just one of her stories in which she was a character – a heroine: brave, unafraid, ready to die for the good of the world. Suddenly, she felt terror.

Here in my dark silent cell, my heart is thumping. I am afraid again. They will come for me soon.

The wheels struck the ground. There was a fierce bumping as the Lysander hurtled over the rough field. The dark shadows of trees whipped by like a smear from a paintbrush. Would they ever stop? They stopped, but the propellers kept spinning. The engine noise sounded dangerously loud.

'Out, out!' they yelled, pushing Noor through the door.

She was already dressed to look like a nursemaid. She was to pretend to be on her way to Paris to look after an old lady. So she was wearing a war-worn but well-tailored suit, a beret over her black short hair and black walking shoes. She would look as if she was on her way back from leave. They tossed her suitcase out to her, shabby and scratched, but hidden within its false lining, under her nurse's apron and cap, were her transmitter and her instructions.

'You will meet Garry,' they had told her. 'Your network is called Prospero. He will take you to them.'

No sooner had she leaped to the ground than the Lysander was already moving again and was sky-borne – before she'd even turned to meet the man standing the shadows.

He grasped her hand in the darkness. '*Viens. Vite!*' He snatched her suitcase with his other hand and began to run, tugging her along. They must get away from the field. Someone may have heard the plane. The Germans could be on their way. Already Noor had a stitch in her side; she was bent double, gasping – but kept running, allowing him to drag her along, pushing her through hedges and over stiles. At last they reached a small clearing. A car was waiting. Someone opened the door. 'Get in.' The case was thrown into the boot, then they were off – driving without lights – and hit the road to Paris.

'Garry!' My heart is thumping again. I call out his name. It has a hollow ring in this dark stone cell. 'Where are you now?'

Where are any of them? Gilbert, Antoine, Marguerite, Valentin. Some are dead. She had only been in Paris a week when the Nazis rounded up nearly all of the cell called Prospero. There was treachery everywhere, but the Gestapo didn't know her yet, so she slipped away and kept up radio contact with London.

She moved from one dreary apartment to another, hanging her aerial out of the windows to pick up signals from London, while trying to evade the direction-finding trucks which roamed the streets listening out for illegal transmissions.

I can still laugh – a croaking, gulping, last-gasp laugh – when I remember one fool of a Nazi coming in on me as I tried to fix up my aerial. He thought it was a washing line and helped me.

● ● ● ●

She lived like this for three months, the only British radio operative in Paris still free, still transmitting to London – staying on air a few minutes at a time, then moving on. A man called 'B' arrived from England to check out what was left of the Resistance.

'Come home with me,' he advised. 'You know you'll be shot if they catch you?'

She refused. 'They don't know me. I can still go on working for you. There's no one else left. You need me.' So 'B' returned without her.

But the Nazis were after her. Somehow they got to know her code name – Madeleine. Someone had betrayed her. She arrived back to her apartment one day to find a Gestapo officer in her room.

'She was like a wild cat,' he had reported later. She fought and bit and tried to get out. 'I had to pull a gun on her.' He phoned for help and other officers arrived They ransacked her room and found her transmitter, notebooks, codes and ciphers. They took her to their headquarters at the Avenue Foch for interrogation.

'Just tell us all you know. Give us names, contacts. Tell us what the British are planning to do.'

'My name is Norah Baker. My number is 9901 – assistant section officer for the Women's Auxiliary Air Force Transport Service,' was all she would tell them.

'You're a fool.' They shook their heads with false pity. You'll soon speak. Take her away.'

She made another desperate attempt to escape by climbing through a window and slithering across the rooftops. But they caught her and dragged her back.

She was now classified as a 'dangerous prisoner'.

● ● ● ●

'They hurt me, Papa. They hurt me so much.'

● ● ● ●

'We already know everything,' sneered the Gestapo. 'Your colleague broke. We know all about the plans. You might as well give in and save yourself more pain.'

'My name is Norah Baker, number 9901...' She refused to give more than her name, rank and number.

Her masters thought she would break in the end. It was part of the plan. She would pass on false information; would tell them there was a plan to invade, that the Allies would land in Calais – not Normandy. But after five weeks of fierce interrogation, she stayed silent.

Love is action; action is knowledge; knowledge is truth; truth is love.

She was put on a train to Karlsruhe in Germany. There she stayed for ten months, in solitary confinement, shackled in chains. In September 1944 she was put on another train. So this is where I am, Papa; Dachau. Not many people walk out alive from here. There are three other women from my section. We will meet for the first time in a few moments. I can hear the first birdsong of dawn. Yes – even in my cell, their song reaches me. I hear footsteps. They are coming.

'Awake! For morning in the bowl of night has flung the stone that put the stars to flight.'

Four women were taken out at dawn to a place all strewn with sand.

● ● ● ●

The sand is stained with blood.

I am a hare.

● ● ● ●

They were told to kneel. Four women – strangers to each other till then – held hands like sisters and knelt down together. An SS man came up behind them and, one by one, shot them dead.

Postscript: Princess Noor Inayat Khan was posthumously awarded the George Cross by the British and the Croix de Guerre by the French.

Real Tears
Celia Rees

Introduction

Soldiers have always sought to protect non-combatants from the brutal realities of war, claiming, in the words of a song from the First World War, that 'They would never believe it.' Even at a time when we think that the camera shows us everything, there are things that we are prevented from seeing. We get only a faint echo of the screaming, a fading after-image of the horror of the immediate experience. No camera can communicate that, or the endurance and courage that soldiers have to display if they are to live with the boredom, terror, disgust and fear that they experience every day as part of the job.

The British public, by contrast, has always had an ambivalent attitude towards serving soldiers, from Rudyard Kipling's Tommy Atkins (who complains in the poem 'Tommy' that the British public has no regard for soldiers during peacetime, but is lavish with empty praise and gratitude during wartime), to the ladies who gave out white feathers to off-duty officers wearing civilian clothing. How much more would this be so for soldiers serving in a war that is unpopular in the first place?

I wanted to write a story about that. What kind of reception might a soldier receive when he comes home on leave from Iraq?

Real Tears

'Can you still do that thing?'

'What? What thing?'

I was having trouble hearing him over the music and everyone talking. He was standing next to me, hands loosely clasped, resting on the bar. His wrists were thick and sunburned. The ring he wore – third finger, left hand – was a heavy gold number, engraved with some kind of insignia. As he talked he turned it round and round.

'You know, that trick. You did it at Jake's party. You're famous for it.' He smiled. Teeth white against his tanned face. I'd forgotten how handsome he was. He was a friend of my brother's, or used to be.

'Oh.' I grinned back, catching his drift. '*That* trick. Now let me think. A trick like that takes concentration.'

I'd perfected it when I was a small child. My brother is older than me. He won all our fights easily and used to tease me without mercy, laughing at my fury. There was only one way to get back at him. I felt the prickling pepper sting and the tears began to well and brim. It is important not to sneeze, or the effect is lost entirely. Then I blink once, twice, so that the tears spill and fall. I felt them find the channels at the side of my nose and imagined them reflecting the light, taking on a silvery glitter. I tasted salt at the corner of my mouth.

He caught a drop from my chin, held it on his fingertip.

'That's a good trick!' He grinned at me, delighted.

I smiled back. I knew it.

I took out a tissue and dabbed my face. I'm the only person I know who can cry at will. No red nose, no puffy eyes. I just look tragic, although it's good to wear waterproof mascara.

'That deserves a drink.' He turned back to the bar. 'What are you having?'

'A glass of white wine, please.'

He got served right away and I was glad he'd stood next to me. I'd been waiting ages. The bar was crowded. A-level results had come out that day. Everyone was out. I was celebrating, rather than drowning my sorrows.

'What are you doing here?' I said, as we found a space to stand. Somewhere to sit was out of the question.

'I'm home for a bit. Thought I'd come out for a drink.' He looked around. 'This place has changed. We used to come here.'

He meant with my brother.

'It hasn't really. Just a different crowd.'

'I guess. I don't know anyone now.' He laughed and drained his pint. 'They make me feel like a grandad. You ready for another?'

'I'm all right, thanks.'

I watched him as he wove his way back to the bar. It would have been easy to make an escape, drift off and join any of half a dozen different groups, but part of me thought that would be rude. He had been my brother's best friend when they were at school, and used to come to our house all the time. He never took any interest in me, of course, but I'd had quite a crush on him. At fifteen, I'd been in love. For certain and forever. I told everyone I was interested only in older men. I may even have written poems. They were at university then; he used to come to our house and hang out in the vacations. I'd drift round on hot summer days, wearing as little as possible, trying to catch his eye. I'd pretend to sunbathe and watch him and my brother doing pull-ups on the bar they'd rigged up between the house and the garage. I didn't think he'd noticed, but he must have done. I'd done the crying trick at my brother's twenty-first. At the end of that summer, there had been a falling-out. I don't remember him coming round much after that.

'Who's the fit guy?' My friend Stephanie bumped my shoulder, making me spill my drink. She'd obviously been celebrating harder than I had. 'Are you keeping him to yourself, or what?'

'I haven't decided.'

'Pass him on to me, if you can't make your mind up. He's hot!' She giggled into her vodka and Coke. 'I'm not the only one who's noticed.'

I followed her line of sight and saw that my ex was ignoring his new girlfriend and staring in our direction. He looked past, frowning hard towards the bar. I had to turn away to hide the smile on my face. That made deciding even easier.

● ● ● ●

'I bought you one anyway.' He gave the glass to me. 'Getting served is murder. Who's this?'

He smiled at Stephanie, who did her special eyelash-fluttering flirty laugh, the one she thinks is really seductive.

'This is Ben.' I introduced them, knowing Stephanie wasn't going anywhere until she knew his name, at the very least.

'It's such a row in here,' she said. 'Why don't we go out to the courtyard? It's just that, oh —' She waved her glass. 'I appear to be empty.'

'What would you like?'

'A Duke Doubler,' she said quickly.

'A Duke what?'

'They'll know behind the bar. Just ask for it.'

It was double shots of white rum, vodka and something else, with that blue stuff to top it off. It came in a fancy glass with parasols.

'OK. Look after my pint.'

'I've always wanted one of those. Might as well make the most of it.' Stephanie took a swig of his beer. 'I bet he's loaded. Officers earn tons of money.'

'How do you know he's a soldier?' I asked.

'Look how short his hair is, and he's built! Besides, he's got that ring. Don't you notice anything? A regimental thing. My uncle's got one like it. You'd make a rubbish detective.'

I knew anyway. That was why he'd fallen out with my brother. Jake is left wing. A trainee journalist on the *Guardian*. He couldn't believe a friend of his could want to join the forces. Ben had said, no problem – and they were no longer friends. And I never said I wanted to be a detective.

Ben came back with Steph's drink and we fought our way out to the courtyard. It was only slightly less packed but most of our friends were there, and at least it was open to the air, not choked with cigarette smoke.

As for the argument, I have to blame Steph. She was the one who told them that he was a soldier. Up to that point, all I'd been concerned about was the fact that he was older. He bought a pitcher of cocktails and beers for the boys and seemed happy enough to hang out with us, but he'd been there, done that and I was worried he could get bored with all the talk of A levels, school and university.

Ginny picked up on his job as soon as the words left Steph's big mouth. She was the one with the most definite views – on everything. Not just the war. She'd gained her clutch of A grades, but did not intend to take her place up yet. She was going on a gap year.

'I'm going to travel,' she said, 'see the world. It's important to see how other people live. Poor people who are less fortunate than we are in the West. After all, it's us who've made them like that. I intend to do what I can to make a difference.'

'Oh yeah?' Steph sneered. She'd heard the speech before and there's not a lot of love lost between her and Ginny. 'And just how is you lying on a beach with Stu going to make the slightest bit of difference to anyone? Please tell me.'

'Because I'm not going to be doing that.' Ginny's voice was as cold as the ice in her glass. 'I'm going to the Middle East. To teach English on the West Bank.'

We all stared at her. That was news. The last plan involved Ginny and her boyfriend, Stu, spending time in Thailand and Cambodia before going to stay with his auntie who owned retail outlets in Brisbane, Australia.

'It's important to put something back.' She glared at Ben. 'Help to repair the damage *some* people are doing in that part of the world.'

'It's dangerous there.' His tone was mild, even affable. 'You be careful.'

'Oh,' she flashed back, 'and who's made it like that? You. You and those like you. Look at Iraq.' I groaned and shut my eyes. Ginny was about to make one of her great leaps of logic. 'What conceivable excuse did you have for invading that country? None at all. Now look what's going on. Children murdered. Innocent people slaughtered.'

'Hey!' He tried a smile. 'I don't do that. I'm in the Engineers, putting back the infrastructure that's been destroyed –'

The smile didn't work.

'By *who*?' Ginny was fairly squeaking with indignation. 'By YOU! Don't you feel the slightest bit *guilty*?'

'Why should I? My job is to help people.'

'Oh, please!' Ginny rolled her eyes. 'Don't even *think* about trying to patronize me. We all know what's happening out there: thousands tortured and killed every day...'

She was shouting across everybody, right into his face. At first, he tried to parry what she said, set out counter-arguments. When that didn't work, he just listened. The more she battered him with words, the more silent he became. He didn't look at her – he didn't look at any of us – he just stared at the whitewashed wall, a distant, abstracted stare, as if there were scenes playing there that only he could see. The bright bloom of flame within roiling oily black smoke; people running in panic and confusion; the moment when the camera pulls back from the scene in the bomb-torn street, swinging up and away from the scrap of burned fabric, the gob of meat, the bloodstained smear that had started the day as a human being. We didn't have to see, but he did. He could smell the charred flesh, hear the screams. Best you don't know, his stare seemed to say. I'm not going to tell you, anyway, because you wouldn't believe me if I did. Hasn't that always been the way of soldiers?

'Yeah.'

'She's right.'

'What are you going to do about it, mate?'

One by one, the others joined in, taking turns to have a go at him.

'Let's leave.' Ginny stood up. 'No point in talking to someone who just won't listen.'

'Yeah. Let's go to Lyle's.'

Lyle's was the local cheesy club. A consensus formed. It was clear Ben and I were not invited.

'I'm not about to win any popularity contests with your friends.' His grin was ironic, but there was a bruised, hurt look about his eyes. The attack had been savage. 'Do you mind? I mean, you can go with them, if you want. Don't feel you have to stay with me…'

'Why should I mind? With a bit of luck I'll never see any of them ever again.'

Steph had been in the toilet for quite a while, probably throwing up. She came back not looking so good.

'Where *is* everybody?'

'They've gone to Lyle's.'

"K. 'S go.'

'D'you think that's a good idea?'

'Prob'ly not.' Stephanie sat down heavily, just avoiding my lap.

'Maybe we better call it a night. I think so, don't you?'

'S'pose.' Steph'll go on till the end, but the Duke Doublers had taken their toll. She knows her limits.

'Here.' Ben stood up, pulling her to a standing position. 'I'd give you a lift, but I've had a bit to drink.'

'She'll be all right. We'll go down to the rank for a cab.'

'I'll come with you.'

Exactly what I was hoping he'd say. A sudden ''Scuse me' from Steph gave me time to make further arrangements. I could say I was staying with her. She'd never remember if I'd been there or not. That's if he asked.

'My folks are away,' he said, right on cue. 'I was wondering after we drop Stephanie off ... I was wondering if you'd like to come back with me.'

'Yes,' I said.

Just like that. He was a really nice guy and he hadn't deserved that kind of going-over. Some part of me wanted to make it up to him. And I still fancied him, I had to admit. All that dreaming on my bed and now it was coming true. It was the kind of chance that doesn't come twice. Unrequited love about to be requited.

'Hadn't you better see about your friend?'

Lost in romantic reverie, I'd forgotten about Stephanie. I found her by the basins looking like Alice Cooper. I wiped the worst of the mascara streaks from her cheeks and made her drink some water.

'How do you feel now?'

'Fine. Jus' fine. He seems like a nice guy. Don' mind Ginny. She's a silly bitch.'

Given the state she was in, that was a long speech.

'Think you can make it?

'Course.'

I helped her out, and then Ben took over. He held her up, walking her all the way down to the taxi stand. There was one cab there, which was lucky.

'OK. In you get.'

Ben opened the door, helping Steph into the back. I was just about to follow her when this guy began to shout.

'That's our effing cab. Get out!'

'You are joking!' Ben shook his head and grinned. 'We were here first!'

The guy grabbed Ben's arm and spun him around. He was smaller than Ben, but he made up for his lack of build with plenty of aggression.

'What did you say?' He was dancing on the pavement, jittering with rage.

'I said, "No way. You're joking."'

'I ain't, mate.'

A bunch of others stepped out from the side of the kebab van.

'I don't want to fight.' Ben put up his hands, palms out. 'I have to warn you, I'm trained in unarmed combat...'

'Oh yeah?'

The guy had been stepping backwards, now he lunged forward fast and hit Ben hard. Then he was gone, his mates running after him.

'You all right?' the taxi driver finally came round from his side of the cab.

'I don't know...'

Ben tried to straighten up but sank to the ground, bent over like a puppet. He pulled his hand from inside his coat and stared.

His face creased, somewhere between grin and grimace, as if he couldn't believe what he was seeing, couldn't believe this was happening.

Steph was out of the cab. Sober in an instant.

'Don't just stand there!' She screamed at me, the taxi driver, the small group gathering. 'Call for an ambulance. Call the police!'

Phones came out. Calls were made. We knelt by Ben, cradling his head, trying to make him comfortable.

'Don't move him too much.' Steph made a pad with her wrap, pressed it against his chest. 'Hold on,' she kept saying to him. 'Hold on.'

But it was too late. She knew it, even as she said it. We looked at each other over his head. I cried then. Real tears.

Author's note: *Violence is everywhere and war is full of savage ironies. The direct inspiration for this story was a news report I read about a young British soldier on leave from Iraq. He was going home to see his mother but never reached his destination. He was murdered while waiting for a bus.*

Worth It
Malorie Blackman

Monday, 28th June

Old Horsey showed me up something rotten today. Sometimes he can be a right cow pat! After taking the register, he started going through the final selections for the doubles tennis tournament against Lichfield School. His shiny, bald head was bent over the list as he read out the first two teams from our year – Sarah and Minty from Mr Knight's class and Paul and Luther from Mrs Hibbert's class. Then Old Horsey lifted his head and narrowed his eyes and looked directly at *me*. My face started to burn, even before he said anything.

'Judith, if I put you down to play as our C team, can you be relied on to be here, or will you be off school again?'

Everyone turned to look at me. If I'd put my head on my desk at that moment, the desk would have caught fire.

'I'll be here sir,' I protested. Old Horsey raised his mega-bushy eyebrows.

'Are you sure? You've been away rather a lot during these last two terms.'

By now all I wanted to do was merge with the paint on the walls and disappear.

'I haven't been bunking off, sir,' I said indignantly. 'It's just that…that I didn't feel well. But I've been here for the last four or five weeks. I'm all right now.'

'Hmm!' Old Horsey scrutinized me, his eyes now just tiny slits in his head.

'Do you *want* to play in the tournament?' he asked.

'Of course I do, sir,' I replied. What a stupid question!

'There's no "of course" about it,' said Old Horsey. 'If you turned up to more of the practice sessions, I *might* think you were taking the game seriously. You could be a very good player if only you'd apply yourself. But like everyone else, you don't want to stay after school. Too eager to play video games at home, I suppose.'

Now was that fair or what? 'Don't say a word, Judith. Not one word,' I told myself. Hard work!

It wasn't my fault that I'd been away from school a few times in the last two terms. It's bad enough not being able to set foot in or out of my house unless I play twenty questions with Mum and Dad first, without getting it in the neck at school too.

Take this morning for example.

Dad was late for work, so all he had time to do was down a cup of coffee and pull on his jacket before he headed out the door. But he still found time to interrogate me.

'Are you all right, Judith?'

'Yes, Dad.'

'Are you sure?'

'Yes, Dad.'

'Drinking plenty?'

'Yes, Dad.'

'You're keeping warm?'

'Dad, it's fifty million degrees outside.'

'You're not getting dehydrated, are you?'

'Dad, give it a rest!'

And then I got exactly the same thing from Mum when she drove me part of the way to school on her way to the train station.

The two of them are driving me nuts! And what about that letter they told me to take to Mr Horsmann? I mean, how *could* they? No way was I going to let him or any of the teachers see that. Imagine telling them what I've got and asking them to look after me. I'm twelve, not two. The way my mum and dad are going on, anyone would think I'm about to kick the bucket at any second. We did fine before any of us found out I had Sickle Cell, so why can't we just pick up where we left off? Why does it have to change everything? I'm so cheesed off. All this fuss, fuss, fussing is driving me right up the wall. Tasha's the only one who treats me the way she's always done. Without Tasha I'd go mental, I'm sure I would.

Where was I? Oh yeah!

Anyway, finally Horsey bent his head to his list again. 'OK Judith, you and Tasha are the C team.'

'Yes!' I punched the air above my head. Tasha elbowed me in the ribs, grinning at me.

Old Horsey looked around.

'Class, this tournament is very important. Lichfield School won the cup from us last year and this time next week, I want it back where it belongs.'

'In Mrs Cookson's office where no-one can even glance at it,' Tasha muttered to me.

'Too right,' I mumbled back.

It wasn't as if any of us could just stroll into the head's office and ask to see it. Old Horsey nodded in my direction. 'So you won't let me down, Judith,' he said.

'I won't, sir,' I answered.

Tasha elbowed my ribs again. I elbowed her back.

I crossed my fingers and scrunched up my toes in my shoes. I crossed my arms and my legs. I even tried looking at my nose so I'd go cross-eyed. 'You're not going to get sick again. You're not…you're not…Not until after the tournament at any rate,' I told myself.

'Judith Stenning, what on earth are you doing?' Old Horsey frowned.

'Er…nothing, sir,' I replied, looking straight at him, all innocent.

The frown lines on his forehead were deep enough to swim in but he didn't say any anything. Tasha elbowed me for a third time.

'Oi! That hurts, you moron,' I hissed. 'Are you trying to break a bone or something?'

'It was only a light tap,' Tasha said.

Tap, my eyeball! Tasha's 'light tap' has left a whopping great bruise on my side. I just hope Mum or Dad don't see it or, knowing them, they'll want to rush me straight to hospital.

God, I hate it when they fuss.

● ● ● ●

I had the strangest dream last night. Maybe it's an omen. I dreamt I was at the tennis tournament on Friday and that our school and Lichfield's were level pegging. Both schools had forty-five points each and there was only one more match left to play. The decider. And guess who had to play it? Yep! Me and Tasha against two of Lichfield's lot.

Everyone gathered around our court. All eyes were on us. No-one said a word. Old Horsey was looking straight at Tasha and me and he didn't even blink. We knew we couldn't make any mistakes.

It was a tough match. It got to one set all and four games all in the third set and then guess what? It was my turn to serve and I served four aces in a row so we won the game. That made Tasha and me five games to four up. Then it was their side to serve. It got to deuce. Then advantage to us. The boy from Lichfield was serving to me and he was *fast*. I could see him winding up for a mega-fast ace. I stepped back a bit. He served. *And I hit it back.*

Straight over the net and past both of them. I scored the winning shot. We won the match.

You should have heard the noise then. Our school was screaming and yelling, even Mr Horsmann's eyes were damp. Our school crowded on to the court and lifted Tasha and me up into the air. Mr Horsmann and some of the other teachers started singing some boring song about 'For they are jolly good fellows'. My classmates started singing, 'You can't touch this' and 'In your face'! It was brilliant.

Then I woke up. It was so real, so clear. I felt so good I didn't even mind that it was a dream after a while. It must be an omen. We're going to win on Friday. And I'm going to have something to do with it. I hope. Maybe.

School wasn't too bad today. Mr Horsmann was more interested in the forthcoming tennis championship than in teaching us anything, which was good because it's far too blazing hot for lessons. He told us that this year, to make sure we get through all the matches before nightfall, only three doubles teams from each year are being allowed to play and each match is only going to consist of one set. Each team gets three points if they win, and one point if they lose. Don't play, no points. That's fair enough. Each team will play three matches. The school with the most points at the end of the tournament gets the cup. I'm looking forward to playing in the tournament so much. I'm sure Tasha and I are going to do well. We're going to be ace!

Tasha and I went for a practice in the park after school. I had to practically go down on my knees to Mum and Tasha had to back me up, but she finally let me go. I swear, she's getting worse. She's almost as bad as Dad now. She gave me a bottle of water to take with me. I ask you!

'If you don't take the water, you can't go,' Mum said.

So I didn't have any choice.

Actually, I was glad after the third game. I felt like I was wilting, so I was glugging back water like nobody's business. Even Tasha needed some.

I'm glad Tasha knows what I've got. At first I was sorry I'd told her. Tasha's a bit of a div and keeping secrets isn't her strong point. But she's kept mine. I was afraid for a while that she'd tell everyone, but she didn't. I still feel a bit guilty about thinking she'd snitch on me. I should have known she wouldn't. Tasha's not like that.

I think that's enough for tonight. I'm sleepy.

Wednesday, 30th June

Tasha and I went for another practice in the park after school. After a couple of games I called a halt.

'We don't want to overdo it,' I said to Tasha.

'What d'you mean?' she asked.

'Well if we practise too much now, we'll be past our best on Friday.'

'But we've only played two games,' Tasha protested.

'I think we should stop now,' I said stubbornly. Tasha ran towards the net and jumped over it. She came running up to me.

'Judith, you're not hurting are you?' she asked suspiciously.

'Of course not,' I replied. 'I hope you're not turning into my mum.'

We walked back home and played video games for a while until Dad was his usual subtle self and said to Tasha, 'Haven't you got a home to go to?' Honestly!

I drank a lot of water when Tasha left. I've even got a bottle of water on the floor next to my bed now. I wish it would cool down a bit. I hate it when it gets this hot. Playing tennis in fifty million degrees is all work and no fun.

My stomach started playing up this evening.

Thursday, 1st July

Mum and Dad started on at me this morning. I was trying to eat my breakfast when all the questions started. I sort of lost my temper.

'How are you feeling, Judith?' Dad asked.

'Are you all right?' said Mum.

'Do you have to keep asking me that?' I said. 'If there was something wrong with me I'd tell you. Stop asking me all the time.'

'Judith, we're only…'

'You're fussing. I hate it when you fuss over me. I'm not ill all the time, you know.'

By now I was angry. I didn't mean to be but that's how it came out.

'That's enough, Judith.' Mum frowned. 'We're only looking after you. We just don't want you to go back into hospital again.'

I leapt out of my chair. Why did we always come back to that? Ever since last September, when I was told that what was causing my stomach pains and the pains in my arms and legs was Sickle Cell, I'd been in hospital three times – which was three times too often.

I've been ill more times than that, but not bad enough to go into hospital. Which is just as well, 'cause I hate it. All those funny peculiar smells like disinfectant and sick and the doctors talking to me like I was an idiot and the nosy grown-ups visiting their own kids, but still stopping at my bed to ask me what I'm in for. I hate it.

'I'm not going into hospital again,' I shouted. 'I'm tired of hospital. I'm tired of drips in my arm and pethidine injections in my bum and an oxygen mask over my face. I'm tired of hurting. I hate having Sickle Cell. Hate it. Hate it.'

'Judith…'

'I've got to go to school,' I interrupted.

And I ran out of the room before Dad could say another word. I grabbed my jacket from off the coat rack and scarpered out the door. I ran and ran, all the way down to the bottom of our road and around the corner. Only then did I give in. I stopped running and clutched my stomach and doubled over. I was almost on my knees with the pain. My eyes were stinging.

'Go away,' I kept saying, over and over.

I couldn't be ill – not now. Not with the tennis tournament only one day away. I just had to hang on for one more day. I forced myself to straighten up. I took lots of deep breaths.

'My stomach doesn't hurt. It doesn't hurt the least bit,' I muttered.

I took one step forward and doubled over again. 'I'm going to play tennis tomorrow. You're not going to stop me,' I told my stomach.

The pain started to ease a bit at that. It really did. It didn't go away completely, but at least I could walk to school now.

I told Tasha that I couldn't practise in the park after school with her because Mum wanted me to come straight home. In the break times and at lunchtime I headed for the nearest water fountain and drank until I felt like a water-filled balloon. Then I made for the library and sat in the coolest bit of it. It was no use. Tasha still found me.

'You *are* hurting, aren't you?' She stood over me, looking really annoyed.

'Don't worry. I'll play tomorrow if it kills me.' I whispered back. 'So you can take that look off your face. I'm not going to let you down.'

'Don't be so stupid, Judith.' Tasha was even more annoyed now. 'If you're hurting, you shouldn't play. It's you I'm thinking about. I couldn't care less about the tennis championship.' She sat down next to me. I glanced around, anxious to make sure that there were no nosy parkers within earshot.

'Tasha, I'll be all right. I just have to take it easy today.'

'You should tell Mr Horsmann…'

'No chance. And if you tell him I'll… I'll…'

'All right, I get the idea,' Tasha said.

We glared at each other.

'So where's it hurting this time?' she asked.

'My stomach.'

'Is it bad?'

'It comes and goes. It's not too bad at the moment.'

'You should tell your mum and dad at least. If you hang about, it'll only get worse,' Tasha said.

I scowled at her. 'What makes you such an expert?'

'You do,' Tasha replied. 'You're nuts! No tennis tournament is worth playing if you don't feel well. Not even Wimbledon!'

'It's not so much the tennis tournament,' I sighed. 'I just…I don't want to spend the rest of my life not doing things because of…because of what I've got. I've got to prove to myself that I can do anything anyone else can do.'

'So how's playing tennis tomorrow when you don't feel well going to prove that?' Tasha asked.

'It just will, that's all.'

'That's the daftest thing I've ever heard.' Tasha snorted. 'If *I* was ill with the flu or chickenpox or something, I wouldn't play tomorrow. So why do you have to play?'

'Because I do. Besides, it's not the same thing. You only get ill once in a blue moon.' I frowned. 'Tasha, if I don't do this now, there'd be no point in me doing any sports or trying anything new ever again. It's like…it's like if I don't play, then I won't do anything because I might get ill. I don't want to have a ready-made excuse that I can use at any time. Once I start doing that then I don't have to try anything, ever again.'

'I don't understand.'

I shrugged. 'Look, I have to play tomorrow. I just *have* to. Besides we're going to win all our matches, I know we are.'

'Oh yeah! And how do you know that?' Tasha asked.

'Don't laugh,' I whispered, 'but I dreamt it. And this dream is going to come true.'

'You dreamt it?' Tasha couldn't believe her ears. I nodded.

Tasha just looked at me and shook her head.

'My partner's gone round the twist,' she sighed. 'That's just great, that is! You're not going to stand on the court tomorrow and say you're a tea pot or a poached egg are you?'

I creased up laughing. That took my mind off my stomach for a while.

I'm going to sign off now. I want to get an early night. My stomach still hurts. I must admit, I'm a bit worried. If the sun blasts down tomorrow like it's been doing all week, then I'm in trouble. Big trouble. But nothing's going to stop me from playing. Absolutely nothing. We're going to *win*.

Friday, 2nd July

I drunk about a pint of water before I went to bed last night, but I still woke up hurting. The pain wasn't too bad. I've been through worse. But it still hurt like hell. I got out of bed and went to have my shower. I'd barely reached my bedroom door, when my stomach let me know that it was there – with a vengeance. A sharp, stabbing pain shot right through me from my navel to my back. It was so bad it made me yelp out. I bit my lip after that, terrified that Mum and Dad had heard. Luckily for me they were downstairs. I had a quick shower and went down for my breakfast. I forced a smile on to my lips, like painting it on. Mum has this way of just looking at me and knowing that something's wrong, so I couldn't risk that. I forced down my breakfast, even though I wasn't the least bit hungry, just so Mum wouldn't get suspicious. Then I picked up my racket and headed out the door. I groaned the moment I stepped out of the house. It was baking hot already. Something told me it wouldn't be getting any cooler. Tasha was coming up the garden path.

'How are you feeling?' she asked.

'Tasha, if you grew a moustache, I could call you Dad,' I told her. She got the message. She shut up about my health after that and we walked to school together. We talked about the tennis tournament and our strategy for each game we were going to play. Basically, if the ball came in my direction, I'd hit it; if it went towards Tasha, she'd hit it. Not difficult at all!

The tennis tournament was to start after Old Horsey took the register. I was glad about that. I wasn't sure if I'd last until the afternoon. My back had started up as well.

At last it was our turn to play. My stomach was getting worse.

'Judith? Judith, are you all right?' Tasha whispered as we walked out on to the court.

I looked at her. I didn't answer. I spun my racket and we won the toss so Tasha decided we should serve first.

I'm not going to go into all the gruesome details. Except to say that we lost, five games to seven. It wasn't a bad game but it wasn't our best either. What made it worse was that I was sure we could've won it if I'd been feeling better. Old Horsey said as much when we came off the court.

'Better luck next time, both of you,' he said, writing down the scores. Then he looked at me, 'And Judith...'

'Yes, sir.'

'Try running for a few more shots. They're not going to come to you, you know.'

'Yes, sir.'

We walked towards the high fence which marked one side of the court where we were to play our next match. Tasha flopped down. Biting down hard on my bottom lip, I gingerly sat down, feeling my way with my hands first.

'It's getting worse, isn't it?' Tasha said quietly. I nodded. My eyes were stinging.

'Judith, I don't like this,' Tasha said unhappily. 'You shouldn't be playing.'

'I'll be all right.'

'Not if you keep playing.' Tasha replied immediately.

'Stop fussing. I hate…'

'It's not fussing. I'm talking sense,' Tasha interrupted. 'You shouldn't be playing. I've a good mind to tell Mr Horsmann.'

I grabbed her arm. 'Don't you dare,' I warned. 'We have to play. It's too late to find someone else to take my place now, and if we don't play we won't get any points.'

'Stuff the points!' Tasha glowered at me.

'We've only got two more matches to play. We'll win the next two.'

Tasha shook her head, but she didn't say anything. She didn't understand. It wasn't the tennis championship I was so concerned about. I just wanted to play. It was silly, I knew, but I *needed* to play.

We had to wait a while for our second match, and it was almost worth the wait. We had a very close set, but in the end the other team won by six games to three. We shook hands at the end of the match like they do on the telly, then we went to find a seat.

I thought we'd get a rest before our third match but nothing doing. Mr Horsmann told us that our third match was to follow straight on from our second.

My stomach wasn't getting any better.

'Tasha, I don't think I can run much,' I told her as we walked out on court again.

'I knew it. I just knew it,' Tasha said furiously. 'We should stop, right this second. If you explain to Mr Horsmann, he'll…'

'No! I'm playing. It's only one more match,' I said.

I remembered the dream I'd had a few nights before. This match we'd win. We had to win just one. And then the cup would be back in our school again.

Tasha and I lost.

No, we didn't just lose. We were thrashed. We were hammered into the ground. We were pulverized. The final score was one game to us, six games to the other pair.

And it was all my fault. I couldn't run for any of the shots, I had trouble lifting my arms to serve… Basically, I was a disaster.

So much for that rotten, stupid dream.

We'd lost – all three matches.

At the end of the match, Mr Horsmann came towards us, his face stony. Sweat was pouring off me. I looked and felt like I'd been swimming in my sports kit rather than playing tennis. My heart was thundering and I felt so sick. I had to struggle to stay on my feet.

'Mr Horsmann, Judith doesn't feel well. Can I take her inside?' Tasha said before Old Horsey could get a word in edgeways. Our teacher took one look at me and obviously saw that Tasha was telling the truth.

'Mrs Hibbert, could you take over the scoring?' he called out. Mrs Hibbert came over and took his clipboard with all the scores on it.

'What's the matter, Judith?' Mr Horsmann frowned.

'I've…I've got Sickle Cell,' I whispered, 'and I'm having a crisis.'

Mr Horsmann's expression changed at once. 'A crisis?'

'That's what it's called when it starts to hurt a lot,' Tasha explained for me.

'I'll give you a piggy back ride to the medical room. Hop on.' Mr Horsmann squatted down, his back towards me.

I put my arms around his neck whilst he held my legs. Riding on Mr Horsmann's back made me want to laugh, even though my insides were killing me. We must have looked like total divs. Tasha fell into step beside us. I looked around. Every game had stopped as everyone started gawking at us. That made me want to laugh too. Only the pain in my stomach stopped me.

'How long have you been feeling unwell?' Mr Horsmann asked.

'A couple of days,' I replied without thinking. Mr Horsmann turned his head.

'Why on earth didn't you say something?' he asked. 'What on earth possessed you to play today when you knew you weren't well?'

'You told me not to let you down. You said we should get the cup back,' I reminded him.

'Nonsense! The cup's certainly not worth your health. We could have found someone else. And even if we couldn't, the tournament would still have gone on. It doesn't rely on just one person. That's the whole point – this is a team tournament. And you know as well as I do that it's an annual event. You could've played for us next year.' Mr Horsmann let go of one of my legs and started tapping me on top of my head. 'Is there *any* grey matter up there at all? Judith, I can't believe you were so stupid.'

'That's what I said to her, sir,' Tasha piped up.

'I wanted to play,' I protested. 'I wanted...' I gasped as another sliver of pain shot right through me.

'Let's get you to the medical room and then I'll call your parents,' said Mr Horsmann.

After that Mr Horsmann nagged and fussed and fussed and nagged over me until Dad arrived. Then Dad took over where Mr Horsmann had left off. Dad drove me home and helped me to bed. I drank lots of water, took some aspirin and tried to sleep. I almost drifted off a couple of times but that was it. The pain grew steadily worse and worse. So much for the aspirin! They did no good at all.

Two hours later, I was curled up in a ball, clutching my stomach and howling. Mum and Dad drove me round the hospital where they took me straight in – again.

That's where I'm writing this from. I haven't got much more time because the nurses are going to switch out the lights at any second. This evening Mum and Dad stayed with me until visiting hours were over. I got Mum to phone Tasha at home and tell her where I was. She came to visit me too. Mum and Dad showed me up something rotten.

'Judith, how many times have I told you not to play games if it's too hot?' Mum said. 'Your ears are made out of flint!'

'Her ears are stuck in her backside,' sniffed Dad. See what I have to put up with, I thought as I looked at Tasha. She smiled at me. Mum and Dad carried on talking to each other about my ears – what they were made of and where they were on my body and such like. Tasha sat on the bed.

'How are you feeling?' she asked. There was that question again. But for once I didn't mind.

'Better now,' I said. 'They've given me some pethidine.'

'What's pethidine like?'

I shrugged. 'It makes you feel a bit sick, so they have to give you an extra injection for that, but I don't mind. As long as the pethidine stops my stomach from hurting.'

It was strange talking with an oxygen mask on. Cool air was whistling up my nose and when I breathed out, it sounded really loud.

'What's that, then?' Tasha pointed to the upside-down bag of clear liquid which ran down a thin tube and into a vein in my arm.

'It's a drip.'

'I know that. What's in it?'

'Saline I think. Salt water,' I answered.

I moved my arm slightly to watch the drip tube swing back and forth.

'Well?' Tasha asked.

'Well what?' I frowned.

'Was it worth it?'

I looked at the drip and listened to the whistling of the oxygen in the mask which covered most of my face and thought about the pethidine jab they'd given me in my bum.

'All things considered, yes it was,' I said at last. 'It was stupid of me to play, but I reckon it was worth it.'

'Why?' Tasha asked.

'Because…because I *played*. Because I was hurting and I still managed to play. Because I tried.'

Tasha shook her head. 'Like I said, absolutely round the twist!' she said. I grinned at her.

'So which school won the tournament? Do you know? Did we win?' I asked.

She grinned back. 'We sure did. It was very close. Our school won by one point.'

The Princess Diaries
Meg Cabot

Tuesday, September 23

Sometimes it seems like all I ever do is lie.

My mom thinks I'm repressing my feelings about this. I say to her, 'No, Mom, I'm not. I think it's really neat. As long as you're happy, I'm happy.'

Mom says, 'I don't think you're being honest with me.'

Then she hands me this book. She tells me she wants me to write down my feelings in this book, since, she says, I obviously don't feel I can talk about them with her.

She wants me to write down my feelings? OK, I'll write down my feelings:

I CAN'T BELIEVE SHE'S DOING THIS TO ME!

Like everybody doesn't *already* think I'm a freak. I'm practically the biggest freak in the entire school. I mean, let's face it: I'm five foot nine, flat-chested, and a freshman. How much *more* of a freak could I be?

If people at school find out about this, I'm dead. That's it. Dead.

Oh, God, if you really do exist, please don't let them find out about this.

There are four million people in Manhattan, right? That makes about two million of them guys. So out of TWO MILLION guys, she has to go out with Mr Gianini. She can't go out with some guy I don't know. She can't go out with some guy she met at D'Agostino's or wherever. Oh, no.

She has to go out with my Algebra teacher.

Thanks, Mom. Thanks a whole lot.

Wednesday, September 24, Fifth Period

Lilly's like, 'Mr Gianini's cool.'

Yeah, right. He's cool if you're Lilly Moscovitz. He's cool if you're good at Algebra, like Lilly Moscovitz. He's not so cool if you're flunking Algebra, like me.

He's not so cool if he makes you stay after school EVERY SINGLE SOLITARY DAY from 2:30 to 3:30 to practise the FOIL method when you could be hanging out with all your friends. He's not so cool if he calls your mother in for a parent/teacher conference to talk about how you're flunking Algebra, then ASKS HER OUT.

And he's not so cool if he's sticking his tongue in your mom's mouth.

Not that I've actually seen them do this. They haven't even been on their first date yet. And I don't think my mom would let a guy put his tongue in her mouth on the first date. At least, I hope not.

I saw Josh Richter stick his tongue in Lana Weinberger's mouth last week. I had this totally close-up view of it, since they were leaning up against Josh's locker, which is right next to mine. It kind of grossed me out.

Though I can't say I'd mind if Josh Richter kissed *me* like that. The other day Lilly and I were at Bigelow's picking up some alpha hydroxy for Lilly's mom, and I noticed Josh waiting at the check-out counter. He saw me and he actually sort of smiled and said, 'Hey'.

He was buying Drakkar Noir, a men's cologne. I got a free sample of it from the salesgirl. Now I can smell Josh whenever I want to, in the privacy of my own home.

Lilly says Josh's synapses were probably misfiring that day, due to heatstroke or something. She said he probably thought

I looked familiar, but couldn't place my face without the cement block walls of Albert Einstein High behind me. Why else, she asked, would the most popular senior in high school say hey to me, Mia Thermopolis, a lowly freshman?

But I know it wasn't heatstroke. The truth is, when he's away from Lana and all his jock friends, Josh is a totally different person. The kind of person who doesn't care if a girl is flat-chested or wears size eight shoes. The kind of person who can see beyond all that, into the depths of a girl's soul. I know because when I looked into his eyes that day at Bigelow's, I saw the deeply sensitive person inside him, struggling to get out.

Lilly says I have an overactive imagination and a pathological need to invent drama in my life. She says the fact that I'm so upset about my mom and Mr G is a classic example.

'If you're that upset about it, just *tell* your mom,' Lilly says. 'Tell her you don't want her going out with him. I don't understand you, Mia. You're always going around, lying about how you feel. Why don't you just assert yourself for a change? Your feelings have worth, you know.'

Oh, right. Like I'm going to bum my mom out like that. She's so totally happy about this date, it's enough to make me want to throw up. She goes around *cooking* all the time. I'm not even kidding. She made pasta for the first time last night in, like, months. I had already opened the Suzie's Chinese take-out menu, and she says, 'Oh, no cold sesame noodles tonight, honey. I made pasta.'

Pasta! My mom made *pasta!*

She even observed my rights as a vegetarian and didn't put any meatballs in the sauce.

I don't understand any of this.

Things To Do:

1. Buy cat litter.
2. Finish FOIL worksheet for Mr G.
3. Stop telling Lilly everything.
4. Go to Pearl Paint: get soft lead pencils, spray mount, canvas stretchers (for Mom).
5. World Civ. report on Iceland (5 pages, double space).
6. Stop thinking so much about Josh Richter.
7. Drop off laundry.
8. October rent (make sure Mom has deposited Dad's cheque!!!).
9. Be more assertive.
10. Measure chest.

Thursday, September 25

In Algebra today all I could think about was how Mr Gianini might put his tongue in my mom's mouth tomorrow night during their date. I just sat there, staring at him. He asked me a really easy question − I swear, he saves all the easy ones for me, like he doesn't want me to feel left out, or something − and I totally didn't even hear it. I was like, 'What?'

Then Lana Weinberger made that sound she always makes and leaned over to me so that all her blonde hair swished onto my desk. I got hit by this giant wave of perfume, and then Lana hissed in this really mean voice:

'FREAK.'

Only she said it like it had more than one syllable. Like it was spelled FUR-REEK.

How come nice people like Princess Diana get killed in car wrecks, but mean people like Lana never do? I don't understand what Josh Richter sees in her. I mean, yeah, she's pretty. But she's so *mean*. Doesn't he *notice*?

Maybe Lana is nice to Josh, though. *I'd* sure be nice to Josh. He is totally the best-looking boy in Albert Einstein High School. A lot of the boys look totally geeky in our school's uniform, which for boys is grey trousers, white shirt, and black sweater; long-sleeved or vest. Not Josh, though. He looks like a model in his uniform. I am not kidding.

Anyway. Today I noticed that Mr Gianini's nostrils stick out A LOT. Why would you want to go out with a guy whose nostrils stick out so much? I asked Lilly this at lunch and she said, 'I've never noticed his nostrils before. Are you gonna eat that dumpling?'

Lilly says I need to stop obsessing. She says I'm taking my anxiety over the fact that this is only our first month in high school and I already have an F in something, and transferring it to anxiety about Mr Gianini and my mom. She says this is called displacement.

It sort of sucks when your best friend's parents are psychoanalysts.

Today after school the Drs Moscovitz were totally trying to analyse me. I mean, Lilly and I were just sitting there playing Boggle. And every five minutes it was like, 'Girls, do you want some Snapple? Girls, there's a very interesting squid documentary on the Discovery channel. And by the way, Mia, how do you feel about your mother starting to date your Algebra teacher?'

I said, 'I feel fine about it.'

Why can't I be more assertive?

But what if Lilly's parents run into my mom at Jefferson Market, or something? If I told them the truth, they'd *definitely* tell her. I don't want my mom to know how weird I feel about this, not when she's so happy about it.

The worst part was that Lilly's older brother Michael overheard the whole thing. He immediately started laughing his head off, even though I don't see anything funny about it.

He went, *'Your* mom is dating Frank Gianini? Ha! Ha! Ha!'

So great. Now Lilly's brother Michael knows.

So then I had to start begging him not to tell anybody. He's in 5th period Gifted and Talented class with me and Lilly, which is the biggest joke of a class, because Mrs Hill, who's in charge of the G & T programme at Albert Einstein's, doesn't care what we do, as long as we don't make too much noise. She hates it when she has to come out of the teachers' lounge, which is right across the hall from the G & T room, to yell at us.

Anyway, Michael is supposed to use 5th period to work on his online webzine, *Crackhead*. I'm supposed to use it for catching up on my Algebra homework.

But anyway, Mrs Hill never checks to see what we're doing in G & T, which is probably good, since mostly what we're all doing is figuring out ways to lock the new Russian kid, who's supposedly this musical genius, in the supply closet, so we don't have to listen to any more Stravinsky on his stupid violin.

But don't think that just because Michael and I are united in our front against Boris Pelkowski and his violin that he'd keep quiet about my mom and Mr G.

What Michael kept saying was, 'What'll you do for me, huh, Thermopolis? What'll you do for me?'

But there's nothing I can do for Michael Moscovitz. I can't offer to do his homework, or anything. Michael is a senior (just like Josh Richter). Michael has gotten all straight As his entire life (just like Josh Richter). Michael will probably go to Yale or Harvard next year (just like Josh Richter).

What could I do for someone like that?

Not that Michael's perfect, or anything. Unlike Josh Richter, Michael is not on the crew team. Michael isn't even on the debate team. Michael does not believe in organized sports, or organized religion, or organized anything, for that matter. Instead, Michael spends almost all of his time in his room. I once asked Lilly what he does in there, and she said she and her parents employ a 'don't ask, don't tell' policy with Michael: They won't ask if he won't tell.

I bet he's in there making a bomb. Maybe he'll blow up Albert Einstein High School as a senior prank.

Occasionally Michael comes out of his room and makes sarcastic comments. Sometimes when he does this he is not wearing a shirt. Even though he does not believe in organized sports, I have noticed that Michael has a really nice chest. His stomach muscles are extremely well-defined.

I have never mentioned this to Lilly.

Anyway, I guess Michael got tired of me offering to do stuff like walk his sheltie, Pavlov, and take his mom's empty Tab cans back to Gristedes for the deposit money, which is his weekly chore. Because in the end, Michael just said, in this disgusted voice, 'Forget it, OK, Thermopolis?' and went back into his room.

I asked Lilly why he was so mad, and she said because he'd been sexually harassing me, but I didn't notice.

How embarrassing! Supposing Josh Richter starts sexually harassing me some day (I wish) and I don't notice? God, I'm so stupid sometimes.

Anyway, Lilly said not to worry about Michael telling his friends at school about my mom and Mr G, since Michael has no friends. Then Lilly wanted to know why I cared about Mr Gianini's nostrils sticking out so much, since I'm not the one who has to look at them, my mom is.

And I said, Excuse me, I have to look at them from 9:55 to 10:55 and from 2:30 to 3:30 EVERY SINGLE DAY, except Saturdays and Sundays and national holidays and the summer. If I don't flunk, that is, and have to go to summer school.

And if they get married, then I'll have to look at them EVERY SINGLE DAY, SEVEN DAYS A WEEK, MAJOR HOLIDAYS INCLUDED.

Define set: collection of objects element or member; belongs to a set

A = (Gilligan, Skipper, Mary Ann) rule specifies each element

A = (x:x is one of the castaways on Gilligan's Island)

Friday, September 26
Lilly Moscovitz's List of Hottest Guys

(compiled during World Civ., with commentary by Mia Thermopolis)

1. *Josh Richter* (agree – six feet of unadulterated hotness. Blond hair, often falling into his clear blue eyes, and that sweet, sleepy smile. Only drawback: he has the bad taste to date Lana Weinberger.)

2. *Boris Pelkowski* (strongly disagree. Just because he played his stupid violin at Carnegie Hall when he was twelve does not make him hot. Plus he tucks his school sweater into his trousers, instead of wearing it out, like a normal person.)

3. *Pierce Brosnan, best James Bond ever* (disagree – I liked Timothy Dalton better.)

4. *Daniel Day Lewis in* Last of the Mohicans (agree – Stay alive, no matter what occurs.)

5. *Prince William of England* (duh)

6. *Leonardo in* Titanic (As if! That is so 1998.)

7. *Mr Wheeton, the crew coach* (hot, but taken. Seen opening the door to the teachers' lounge for Mademoiselle Klein.)

8. *That guy in that jeans ad on that giant billboard in Times Square* (totally agree. Who IS that guy? They should give him his own TV series.)

9. *Dr Quinn, Medicine Woman's boyfriend* (whatever happened to him? He was hot!)
10. *Joshua Bell, the violinist* (totally agree. It would be so cool to date a musician – just not Boris Pelkowski.)

Later on Friday

I was measuring my chest and totally not thinking about the fact that my mom was out with my Algebra teacher when my dad called. I don't know why, but I lied and told him Mom was at her studio. Which is so weird, because obviously, Dad knows Mom dates. But for some reason, I just couldn't tell him about Mr Gianini.

This afternoon during my mandatory review session with Mr Gianini I was sitting there practising the FOIL method (first, outside, inside, last; first, outside, inside, last – Oh my God, when am I ever going to have to actually use the FOIL method in real life? WHEN???) and all of a sudden Mr Gianini said, 'Mia, I hope you don't feel, well, uncomfortable about my seeing your mother socially.'

Only for some reason for a second I thought he said SEXUALLY, not socially. And then I could feel my face getting totally hot. I mean like BURNING. And I said, 'Oh, no, Mr Gianini, it doesn't bother me at all.'

And Mr Gianini said, 'Because if it bothers you, we can talk about it.'

I guess he must have figured out I was lying, since my face was so red.

But all I said was, 'Really, it doesn't bother me. I mean, it bothers me a LITTLE, but really, I'm fine with it. I mean, it's just a date, right? Why get upset about one measly date?'

That was when Mr Gianini said, 'Well, Mia, I don't know if it's going to be one measly date. I really like your mother.'

And then, I don't even know how, but all of a sudden I heard myself saying, 'Well, you better. Because if you do anything to make her cry, I'll kick your butt.'

Oh my God! I can't even believe I said the word butt to a teacher! My face got even REDDER after that, which I wouldn't have thought possible. Why is it that the only time I can tell the truth is when it's guaranteed to get me into trouble?

But I guess I *am* feeling sort of weird about the whole thing. Maybe Lilly's parents were right.

Mr Gianini, though, was totally cool. He smiled in this funny way and said, 'I have no intention of making your mother cry, but if I ever do, you have my permission to kick my butt.'

So that was OK, sort of.

Anyway, Dad sounded really weird on the phone. But then again, he always does. Transatlantic phone calls suck because I can hear the ocean swishing around in the background and it makes me all nervous, like the fish are listening, or something. Plus Dad didn't even want to talk to me. He wanted to talk to Mom. I suppose somebody died, and he wants Mom to break it to me gently.

Maybe it was Grandmere. Hmmm...

My breasts have grown exactly *none* since last summer. Mom was totally wrong. I did *not* have a growth spurt when I turned fourteen, like she did. I will probably *never* have a growth spurt, at least not on my chest. I only have growth spurts UP, not OUT. I am now the tallest girl in my class.

Now if anybody asks me to the Cultural Diversity Dance next month (yeah, right) I won't be able to wear a strapless dress, because there isn't anything on my chest to hold it up.

Saturday, September 27

I was asleep when my mom got home from her date last night (I stayed up as late as I could, because I wanted to know what happened, but I guess all that measuring wore me out), so I didn't get to ask her how it went until this morning when I went out into the kitchen to feed Fat Louie. Mom was up already, which was weird, because usually she sleeps later than me, and *I'm* a teenager, *I'm* supposed to be the one sleeping all the time.

But Mom's been depressed ever since her last boyfriend turned out to be a Republican.

Anyway, she was in there, humming in a happy way and making pancakes. I nearly died of shock to see her actually cooking something so early in the morning, let alone something vegetarian.

Of course she had a fabulous time. They went to dinner at Monte's (not too shabby, Mr G!) and then walked around the West Village and went to some bar and sat outside in the back garden until nearly two in the morning, just talking. I kind of tried to find out if there'd been any kissing, particularly of the tongue-in-mouth variety, but my mom just smiled and looked all embarrassed.

OK. Gross.

They're going out again this week.

I guess I don't mind, if it makes her this happy.

Today Lilly is shooting a spoof of the movie *The Blair Witch Project* for her TV show, *Lilly Tells It Like It Is*. *The Blair Witch Project* is about some kids who go out into the woods to find a witch, and end up disappearing. All that's found of them is film footage and some piles of sticks. Only instead of *The Blair Witch Project*, Lilly's version is called *The Green Witch Project*. Lilly intends to take a hand-held camera down to Washington Square Park and film the tourists who come up to us and ask if we know how to get to Green Witch Village (it's actually Greenwich Village – you're not supposed to pronounce the *w* in Greenwich. But people from out of town always say it wrong).

Anyway, as tourists come up and ask us which way to Green Witch Village, we are supposed to start screaming and run away in terror. All that will be left of us by the end, Lilly says, is a little pile of Metrocards. Lilly says after the show is aired, no one will ever think of Metrocards the same way.

I said it was too bad we don't have a real witch. I thought we could get Lana Weinberger to play her, but Lilly said that would be typecasting. Plus then we'd have to put up with Lana all day, and nobody would want that. Like she'd even show up, considering how she thinks we're the most unpopular girls in the whole school. She probably wouldn't want to tarnish her reputation by being seen with us.

Then again, she's so vain, she'd probably jump at the chance to be on TV, even if it *is* only a public access channel.

After filming was over for the day, we saw the Blind Guy crossing Bleecker. He had a new victim, this totally innocent German tourist who had no idea that the nice blind man she was helping to cross the street was going to feel her up as soon as they got to the other side, then pretend like he hadn't done it on purpose.

Just my luck, the only guy who's ever felt me up (not that there's anything to feel) was BLIND.

Lilly says she's going to report the Blind Guy to the 6th Precinct. Like they would care. They've got more important things to worry about. Like catching murderers.

Things To Do:

1.   Get cat litter.
2.   Make sure Mom sent out rent cheque.
3.   Stop lying.
4.   Proposal for English paper.
5.   Pick up laundry.
6.   Stop thinking about Josh Richter.

Sunday, September 28

My dad called again today, and this time, Mom really *was* at her studio, so I didn't feel so bad about lying last night, and not telling him about Mr Gianini. He sounded all weird on the phone again so finally I was like, 'Dad, is Grandmere dead?' and he got all startled and said, 'No, Mia, why would you think that?'

And I told him it was because he sounded so weird, and he was all, 'I don't sound weird,' which was a lie, because he DID sound weird. But I decided to let it drop and I talked to him about Iceland, because we're studying Iceland in World Civ. Iceland has the world's highest literacy rate, because there's nothing to do there but read. They also have these natural hot springs, and everybody goes swimming in them. Once, the opera came to Iceland, and every show was sold out and something like 98 per cent of the population attended. Everybody knew all the words to the opera and went around singing it all day.

I would like to live in Iceland some day. It sounds like a fun place. Much more fun than Manhattan, where people sometimes spit at you for no reason.

But Dad didn't seem all that impressed by Iceland. I suppose by comparison, Iceland does make every other country look lucky. The country Dad lives in is pretty small, though. I would think if the opera went there, about 80 per cent of the population would attend, which would certainly be something to be proud of.

I only shared this information with him because he is a politician, and I thought it might give him some ideas about how to make things better in Genovia, where he lives. But I guess Genovia doesn't need to be better. Genovia's number one import is tourists. I know this because I had to do a fact sheet on every country in Europe in the seventh grade, and Genovia was right up there with Disneyland as far as income from the tourist trade is concerned. That's probably why people in Genovia don't have to pay taxes: the government already has enough money. This is called a principality. The only other one is Monaco. My dad says we have a lot of cousins in Monaco, but so far I haven't met any of them, not even at Grandmere's.

I suggested to Dad that next summer, instead of spending it with him and Grandmere at Grandmere's chateau in France, we go to Iceland. We'd have to leave Grandmere at Miragnac, of course. She'd hate Iceland. She hates any place where you can't order up a decent Sidecar, which is her favourite drink, twenty-four hours a day.

All Dad said was, 'We'll talk about that some other time,' and hung up.

Mom is so right about him.

Absolute value: the distance that a given number is from zero on a number line ... always a positive

Monday, September 29, G & T

Today I watched Mr Gianini very closely for signs that he might not have had as good a time on his date with my mom as my mom did. He seemed to be in a really good mood, though. During class, while we were working on the quadratic formula (what happened to FOIL? I was just starting to get the hang of it, and all of a sudden there's some NEW thing: No *wonder* I'm flunking), he asked if anybody had gone out for a part in the fall musical, *My Fair Lady*.

Then later he said, in the way he does when he gets excited about something, 'You know who would be a good Eliza Dolittle? Mia, I think you would.'

I thought I would totally die. I know Mr Gianini was only trying to be nice – I mean, he is dating my mom, after all – but he was SO far off: first of all, because of course they already held auditions, and even if I could've gone out for a part (which I couldn't, because I'm flunking Algebra, hello, Mr Gianini, remember?) I NEVER would've gotten one, let alone the LEAD. I can't sing. I can barely even *talk*.

Even Lana Weinberger, who always got the lead in junior high, didn't get the lead. It went to some senior girl. Lana plays a maid, a spectator at the Ascot Races, and a Cockney hooker. Lilly is House Manager. Her job is to flick the lights on and off at the end of intermission.

I was so freaked out by what Mr Gianini said, I couldn't even *say* anything. I just sat there and felt myself turning all red. Maybe that was why later, when Lilly and I went by my locker at lunch, Lana, who was there waiting for Josh, was all, 'Oh, hello, *Amelia,*' in her snottiest voice, even though nobody has called me Amelia (except Grandmere) since kindergarten, when I asked everybody not to.

Then, as I bent over to get my money out of my backpack, Lana must have got a good look down my blouse, because all of a sudden she goes, 'Oh, how sweet. I see we still can't fit into a bra. Might I suggest Band-Aids?'

I would have hauled off and slugged her – well, probably not: the Drs Moscovitz say I have issues about confrontation – if Josh Richter hadn't walked up AT THAT VERY MOMENT. I knew he totally heard, but all he said was, 'Can I get by here?' to Lilly, since she was blocking his path to his locker.

I was ready to go slinking down to the cafeteria and forget the whole thing – God, that's all I need, my lack of chest pointed out *right in front* of Josh Richter! – but Lilly couldn't leave well enough alone. She got all red in the face and said to Lana, 'Why don't you do us all a favour and go curl up some place and die, Weinberger?'

Well, nobody tells Lana Weinberger to go curl up some place and die. I mean, nobody. Not if they don't want their name written up all over the walls of the Girls' Room. Not that this would be such a heinous thing – I mean, no boys are going to see it in the Girls' Room – but I sort of like keeping my name off walls, for the most part.

But Lilly doesn't care about things like that. I mean, she's short and sort of round and kind of resembles a pug, but she totally doesn't care how she looks. I mean, she has her own TV show, and guys call in all the time and say how ugly they think she is, and ask her to lift her shirt up (*she* isn't flat-chested. She wears a C-cup already) and she just laughs and laughs.

Lilly isn't afraid of anything.

So when Lana Weinberger started in on her for telling her to curl up and die, Lilly just blinked up at her and was like, 'Bite me.'

The whole thing would have escalated into this giant girl fight – Lilly has seen every single episode of *Xena, Warrior Princess,* and can kick-box like nobody's business – if Josh Richter hadn't slammed his locker door closed and said, 'I'm outta here,' in a disgusted voice. That was when Lana just dropped it like a hot potato and scooted after him, going, 'Josh, wait up. Wait up, Josh!'

Lilly and I just stood there looking at each other like we couldn't believe it. I still can't. Who *are* these people, and why do I have to be incarcerated with them on a daily basis?

Homework:
Algebra: Problems 1-12, pg. 79
English: Proposal

World Civ.: questions at end of Chapter 4
G & T: none
French: use avoir in neg. sentence, rd. lessons one to three, pas de plus
Biology: none

B = (x:x is an integer)
D = (2,3,4)
4ED
5ED
E = (x:x is an integer greater than 4 but less than 258)

Tuesday, September 30

Something really weird just happened. I got home from school, and my mom was there (she's usually at her studio all day during the week). She had this funny look on her face, and then she went, 'I have to talk to you.'

She wasn't humming any more, and she hadn't cooked anything, so I knew it was serious.

I was kind of hoping Grandmere was dead, but I knew it had to be much worse than that, and I was worried something had happened to Fat Louie, like he'd swallowed another sock. The last time he did that, the vet charged us $1,000 to remove the sock from his small intestines, and he walked around with a funny look on his face for about a month.

Fat Louie, I mean. Not the vet.

But it turned it wasn't about my cat, it was about my dad. The reason my dad kept on calling was because he wanted to tell us that he just found out, because of his cancer, that he can't have any more kids.

Cancer is a scary thing. Fortunately, the kind of cancer my dad had was pretty curable. They just had to cut off the cancerous part, and then he had to have chemo, and after a year, so far, the cancer hasn't come back.

Unfortunately, the part they had to cut off was...

Ew, I don't even like writing it.

His *testicle*.

GROSS!

It turns out that when they cut off one of your testicles, and then give you chemo, you have, like, a really strong chance of becoming sterile. Which is what my dad just found out he is.

Mom says he's really bummed out. She says we have to be very understanding of him right now, because men have needs, and one of them is the need to feel progenitively omnipotent.

What I don't get is, what's the big deal? What does he need more kids for? He already has me! Sure, I only see him summers and at Christmastime, but that's enough, right? I mean, he's pretty busy, running Genovia. It's no joke, trying to make a whole country, even one that's only a mile long, run smoothly. The only other things he has time for besides me are his girlfriends. He's always got some new girlfriend slinking around. He brings them with him when we go to Grandmere's place in France in the summer. They always drool all over the pools and the stables and the waterfall and the twenty-seven bedrooms and the ballroom and the vineyard and the farm and the airstrip.

And then he dumps them a week later.

I didn't know he wanted to *marry* one of them, and have kids.

I mean, he never married my mom. My mom says that's because at the time, she rejected the bourgeois mores of a society that didn't even accept women as equals to men and refused to recognize her rights as an individual.

I kind of always thought that maybe my dad just never asked her.

Anyway, my mom says Dad is flying here to New York tomorrow to talk to me about this. I don't know *why*. I mean, it doesn't have anything to do with *me*. But when I went to my mom, 'Why does Dad have to fly all the way over here to talk to me about how he can't have kids?' she got this funny look on her face, and started to say something, and then she stopped.

Then she just said, 'You'll have to ask your father.'

This is bad. My mom only says 'Ask your father' when I want to know something she doesn't feel like telling me, like why people sometimes kill their own babies and how come Americans eat so much red meat and read so much less than the people of Iceland.

Note to self: Look up the words *progenitive, omnipotent,* and *mores*

distributive law
5x + 5y − 5
5(x + y − 1)

Distribute WHAT??? FIND OUT BEFORE QUIZ!!!

Wednesday, October 1

My dad's here. Well, not here in the loft. He's staying at the Plaza, as usual. I'm supposed to go see him tomorrow, after he's 'rested'. My dad rests a lot, now that he's had cancer. He stopped playing polo too. But I think that's because one time a horse stepped on him.

Anyway, I hate the Plaza. Last time my dad stayed there, they wouldn't let me in to see him because I was wearing shorts. The lady who owns the place was there, they said, and she doesn't like to see people in cut-offs in the lobby of her fancy hotel. I had to call my dad from a house phone, and ask him to bring down a pair of trousers. He just told me to put the concierge on the phone, and the next thing you know, everybody was apologizing to me like crazy. They gave me this big basket filled with fruit and chocolate. It was cool. I didn't want the fruit, though, so I gave it to a homeless man I saw on the subway on my way back down to the Village. I don't think the homeless man wanted the fruit either, since he threw it all in the gutter, and just kept the basket to use as a hat.

I told Lilly about what my dad said, about not being able to have kids, and she said that was very telling. She said it revealed that my dad still has unresolved issues with his parents, and I said, 'Well, duh. Grandmere is a *huge* pain in the ass.'

Lilly said she couldn't comment on the veracity of that statement, since she'd never met my grandmother. I've been asking if I could invite Lilly to Miragnac for, like, years, but Grandmere always says no. She says young people give her migraines.

Lilly says maybe my dad is afraid of losing his youth, which many men equate with losing their virility. I really think they should move Lilly up a grade, but she says she likes being a freshman. She says this way, she has four whole years to make observations on the adolescent condition in post–Cold War America.

The 3rd power of x is called cube of x – negative numbers have no sq root

Starting today I will:
1. Be nice to everyone, whether I like him/her or not.
2. Stop lying all the time about my feelings.
3. Stop forgetting my Algebra notebook.
4. Keep my comments to myself.
5. Stop writing my Algebra notes in my journal.

Notes from G & T

Lilly – I can't stand this. When is she going to go back to the teachers' lounge?

Maybe never. I heard they were shampooing the carpet today. God, he is so CUTE.

Who's cute?

BORIS!

He isn't cute. He's gross. Look what he did to his sweater. Why does he DO that?

You're so narrow-minded.

I am NOT narrow-minded. But someone should tell him that in America, we don't tuck in our sweaters.

Well, maybe in Russia they do.

But this isn't Russia. Also, someone should tell him to learn a new song. If I have to hear that requiem for dead King Whoever *one* more time…

You're just jealous, because Boris is a musical genius, and you're flunking Algebra.

Lilly, just because I am flunking Algebra does NOT mean I'm stupid.

OK, OK. What is wrong with you today?

NOTHING!!!!!

slope: slope of a line denoted m is $m = \dfrac{y2 - y1}{x2 - x1}$

Find equation of line with slope = 2

Find the degree of slope to Mr G's nostrils

Thursday, October 2,
Ladies' Room at the Plaza Hotel

Well.

I guess now I know why my dad is so concerned about not being able to have more kids.

BECAUSE HE'S A PRINCE!!!

Geez! How long did they think they could keep something like *that* from me?

Although, come to think of it, they managed for a pretty long time. I mean, I've BEEN to Genovia. Miragnac, where I go every summer, and also most Christmases, is the name of my grandmother's house in France. It is actually on the border of France, right near Genovia, which is between France and Italy. I've been going to Miragnac ever since I was born. Never with my mother, though. Only with my dad. My mom and dad have never lived together. Unlike a lot of kids I know, who sit around wishing their parents would get back together after they get divorced, I'm perfectly happy with this arrangement. My parents broke up before I was ever born, although they have always been pretty friendly to one another. Except when my dad is being moody, that is, or my mom is being a flake, which she can be, sometimes. Things would majorly suck, I think, if they lived together.

Anyway, Genovia is where my grandmother takes me to shop for clothes at the end of every summer, when she's sick of looking at my overalls. But nobody ever mentioned anything about my dad being a PRINCE.

Come to think of it, I did that fact sheet on Genovia two years ago, and I copied down the name of the royal family, which is Renaldo. But even then I didn't connect it with my *dad*. I mean, I know his name is Phillipe Renaldo. But the name of the Prince of Genovia was listed in the encyclopedia I used as Artur Christoff Phillipe Gerard Grimaldi Renaldo.

And that picture of him must have been totally old. Dad hasn't had any hair since before I was born (so when he had chemo, you couldn't even tell, since he was practically bald anyway). The picture of the Prince of Genovia showed someone with A LOT of hair, sideburns, and a moustache too.

I guess I can see now how Mom might have gone for him, back when she was in college. He was something of a hottie.

But a PRINCE? Of a whole COUNTRY? I mean, I knew he was in politics, and of course I knew he had money – how many kids at my school have summer homes in France? Martha's Vineyard, maybe, but not *France* – but a PRINCE?

So what I want to know is, if my dad's a prince, how come I have to learn Algebra?

I mean, seriously.

I don't think it was such a good idea for Dad to tell me he was a prince in the Palm Court at the Plaza. First of all, we almost had a repeat performance of the shorts incident: the doorman wouldn't even let me in at first. He said, 'No minors unaccompanied by an adult', which totally blows that whole *Home Alone II* movie, right?

And I was all, 'But I'm supposed to meet my dad –'

'No minors,' the doorman said again, 'unaccompanied by an adult.'

This seemed totally unfair. I wasn't even wearing shorts. I was wearing my uniform from Albert Einstein's. I mean, pleated skirt, knee socks, the whole thing. OK, maybe I was wearing Doc Martens, but come on! I practically WAS that kid Eloise, and she supposedly ruled the Plaza.

Finally, after standing there for, like, half an hour, saying, 'But my dad ... but my dad ... but my dad ...' the concierge came over and asked, 'Just who *is* your father, young lady?'

As soon as I said his name, they let me in. I realize now that's because even THEY knew he was a prince. But his own daughter, his own daughter nobody tells!

Dad was waiting at a table. High tea at the Plaza is supposed to be this very big deal. You should *see* all the German tourists snapping pictures of themselves eating chocolate chip scones. Anyway, I used to get a kick out of it when I was a little girl, and since my dad refuses to believe fourteen is not little any more, we still meet there when he's in town. Oh, we go other places too. Like we always go to see *Beauty and the Beast,* my all-time favourite Broadway musical, I don't care what Lilly says about Walt Disney and his misogynistic undertones. I've seen it seven times.

So has my dad. His favourite part is when the dancing forks come out.

Anyway, we're sitting there drinking tea and he starts telling me in this very serious voice that he's the Prince of Genovia, and then this terrible thing happens:

I get the hiccups.

This only happens when I drink something hot and then eat bread. I don't know why. It had never happened at the Plaza before, but all of a sudden, my dad is like, 'Mia, I want you to know the truth. I think you're old enough now, and the fact is, now that I can't have any more children, this will have a tremendous impact on your life, and it's only fair I tell you. I am the Prince of Genovia.'

And I was all, 'Really, Dad?' *Hiccup.*

'Your mother has always felt very strongly that there wasn't any reason for you to know, and I agreed with her. I had a very... well, *unsatisfactory* childhood –'

He's not kidding. Life with Grandmere couldn't have been any *picque-nicque. Hiccup.*

'I agreed with your mother that a palace is no place to raise a child.' Then he started muttering to himself, which he always does whenever I tell him I'm a vegetarian, or the subject of

Mom comes up. 'Of course, at the time I didn't think she intended to raise you in a *bohemian artist's loft* in *Greenwich Village,* but I will admit that it doesn't seem to have done you any harm. In fact, I think growing up in New York City instilled you with a healthy amount of scepticism about the human race at large—'

Hiccup. And he had never even *met* Lana Weinberger.

'– which is something I didn't gain until college, and I believe is partly responsible for the fact that I have such a difficult time establishing close interpersonal relationships with women…'

Hiccup.

What I'm trying to say is, your mother and I thought by not telling you, we were doing you a favour. The fact was, we never envisioned that an occasion might arise in which you might succeed to the throne. I was only twenty-five when you were born. I felt certain I would meet another woman, marry her, and have more children. But now, unfortunately, that will never be. So, the fact is, you, Mia, are the heir to the throne of Genovia.'

I hiccuped again. This was getting embarrassing. These weren't little lady-like hiccups, either. They were huge, and made my whole body go sproinging up out of my chair, like I was some kind of five-foot-nine frog. They were loud too. I mean *really* loud. The German tourists kept looking over, all giggly and stuff. I knew what my dad was saying was super-serious, but I couldn't help it, I just kept hiccuping! I tried holding my breath and counting to thirty – I only got to ten before I hiccuped again. I put a sugar cube on my tongue and let it dissolve. No go. I even tried to scare myself, thinking about my mom and Mr Gianini French kissing – even *that* didn't work.

Finally, my dad was like, 'Mia? Mia, are you listening? Have you heard a word I said?'

I said, 'Dad, can I be excused for a minute?'

He looked sort of pained, like his stomach hurt him, and he slumped back in his chair in this defeated way, but he said, 'Go ahead', and gave me five dollars to give to the washroom attendant, which I of course put in my pocket. Five bucks for the washroom attendant! Geez, my whole allowance is ten bucks a week!

I don't know if you've ever been to the Ladies' Room at the Plaza, but it's like totally the nicest one in Manhattan. It's all pink and there are mirrors and little couches everywhere, in case you look at yourself and feel the urge to faint from your beauty or something. Anyway, I banged in there, hiccuping like a maniac, and all these women in these fancy hairdos looked up, annoyed at the interruption. I guess I made them mess up their lip-liner, or something.

I went into one of the stalls, each of which, besides a toilet, has its own private sink with a huge mirror and a dressing table, with a little stool with tassels hanging off it. I sat on the stool and concentrated on not hiccuping any more. Instead, I concentrated on what my dad had said:

He's the Prince of Genovia.

A lot of things are beginning to make sense now. Like how when I fly to France, I just walk onto the plane from the terminal, but when I get there, I'm escorted off the plane before everyone else and get taken away by limo to meet my dad at Miragnac.

I always thought that was because he had Frequent Flyer privileges.

I guess it's because he's a prince.

And then there's that fact that whenever Grandmere takes me shopping in Genovia, she always takes me either before the stores are officially open, or after they are officially closed. She calls ahead to ensure we will be let in, and no one has ever said no.

In Manhattan, if my mother had tried to do this, the clerks at the Gap would have fallen over from laughing so hard.

And when I'm at Miragnac, I notice that we never go out to eat anywhere. We always have our meals there, or sometimes we go to the neighbouring chateau, Mirabeau, which is owned by these nasty British people who have a lot of snotty kids who say things like, 'That's rot', to one another. One of the younger girls, Nicole, is sort of my friend, but then one night she told me this story about how she was Frenching a boy and I didn't know what Frenching was. I was only eleven at the time, which is no excuse, because so was she. I just thought Frenching was some weird British thing, like toad-in-the-hole, or air raids, or something. So then I mentioned it at the dinner table in front of Nicole's parents, and after that, all those kids stopped talking to me.

I wonder if the Brits know that my dad is the Prince of Genovia. I bet they do. God, they must have thought I was mentally retarded, or something.

Most people have never heard of Genovia. I know when we had to do our fact sheets, none of the other kids ever had. Neither had my mother, she says, before she met my dad. Nobody famous ever came from there. Nobody who was born there ever invented anything, or wrote anything, or became a movie star. A lot of Genovians, like my grandpa, fought against the Nazis in World War II, but other than that, they aren't really known for anything.

Still, people who *have* heard of Genovia like to go there, because it's so beautiful. It's very sunny nearly all the time, with the snow-capped Alps in the background, and the crystal blue Mediterranean in front of it. It has a lot of hills, some of which are as steep as the ones in San Francisco, and most of which have olive trees growing on them. The main export of Genovia,

I remember from my fact sheet, is olive oil, the really expensive kind my mom says only to use for salad dressing.

There's a palace there too. It's kind of famous because they filmed a movie there, once, a movie about the three Musketeers. I've never been inside, but we've driven by it before, me and Grandmere. It's got all these turrets and flying buttresses and stuff.

Funny how Grandmere never mentioned having *lived* there all those times we drove past it.

My hiccups are gone. I think it's safe to go back to the Palm Court.

I'm going to give the washroom attendant a dollar, even though she didn't attend me.

Hey, I can afford it: my dad's a prince!

Julie and Me and Michael Owen Makes Three

Alan Gibbons

1

Tuesday 20th June 2000

10.40 a.m.

'Who's that?'

What's that might have been a better way of putting it. What I'm looking at is not so much a girl as a creature from another world. It's as though I've just been born again and suddenly I know what life is for.

'Who *is* that?'

My question is directed at my best mate Bobby Quinn. The way I say it makes his head snap round. I've gone all gaspy and urgent and breathless and he wants to know why. Probably thinks I've plugged myself into the electric mains or something. He joins me staring through the little oblong window in the sports hall door.

'Which one?'

What does he mean, which one? That one. The one with the hair and the shape and the grace.

The one.

'Over there, in blue.'

'Oh her. That's Julie Carter. She's new. She's in my maths set.'

That does it, I've got to work harder in maths! I'm in the second set. Bobby's in top…with Julie.

'Where's she from?'

Spirited from Wonderland...wafted here from Paradise... newly materialised from the planet Wow?

'Huyton. Just moved up from Page Moss.'

'You seem to know a lot about her,' I say, my eyes narrowing with suspicion. I don't believe it, I only saw her for the first time a minute ago and I'm jealous already.

'I talk to people,' says Bobby with a shrug. '*I'm* sociable.'

'*I* can be sociable,' I protest.

No, scrub that. I can't. I've never been more than a couple of steps above the hard core nerds. I'm often awkward talking to the other lads in my year, but with girls I'm completely tongue-tied and hopeless. I heard somewhere that the average tongue weighs six ounces – from Bobby probably. He's a mine of useless information. So if your average tongue weighs in at a bantamweight six ounces, how come mine swells to a mouth-clogging, word-dumbing, heavyweight ten pounds? It's like talking with a boa constrictor in your mouth.

'Fancy her, do you?' Bobby asks.

Fancy her?

Fancy her!

That's not the word for what I'm feeling. It doesn't even come close. My skin has gone hot and prickly. My heart is break-dancing in my ribcage. My mouth is as dry as sandpaper. I'm Mount Vesuvius and molten lava is surging up my oesophagus. What's more, for the first time in my life I actually understand what people mean when they say they've got butterflies in their tummy. Butterflies! What I've got is a swarm of enraged hornets.

'Why don't you ask her out?'

I stare at Bobby. Doesn't he understand what he's saying? Ask her out! This vision in blue. It takes me all my time to ask a girl to pass the salt in the canteen. So how exactly do I go about asking somebody as amazing as Julie to go out with me? She isn't just *a* girl. Suddenly, she's *all* girls.

'I couldn't.'

'Course you could. She's only a girl.'

Only!

It's all right for Bobby. He must have kissed the Blarney stone when he was little. No, he swallowed the thing whole. He could charm a fish out of the sea, could Bobby. He's popular with everybody; the teachers, the other boys, even the girls. He asked Caitlin Brady out at the end of last term. I watched him do it. He just marched up to her and popped the question. She's good-looking too. Not one of your needy, desperate girls. She agreed right away. They've been going steady ever since. He doesn't seem to have any problem chatting up girls. He calls it the Nike technique. Just do it. And if they say no – what the heck – there are plenty more fish in the sea. Their loss, that's Bobby's philosophy. He's got self-confidence to burn.

'She wouldn't give me a second glance,' I stammer. 'I mean, just look at her.'

Bobby looks. 'Yeah, she's nice.'

Nice!

She's gorgeous.

For starters, she's tall. Oh my God, she's probably taller than I am, and what girl wants to be seen out with a midget? I can actually feel myself shrinking as I stand here. She's not skinny, though. No way, she's curvy. Sturdy-looking. Do you say that about girls, sturdy? Listen to me, will you, when it comes to the dating game I don't even know the vocabulary. She's – what's the right word? – sleek. Yes, that's spot on. Julie Carter is sleek. Tall, curvy, athletic and *sleek*. Then there's her hair. It's long and black and glossy. She's got it in one long braid down her back and it skips and jumps as she runs down the crash mat. Look at her, you can see every muscle moving in her legs. She's amazing.

'You have got it bad, haven't you?'

Bobby's right there. I've never felt anything like this. Except maybe that May night in Barcelona when Peter Schmeichel lifted the Champions League trophy and sealed the treble. That was the same sort of thrill. The feeling that makes you clench your fists and yell: Yiss!

But this is different. That was about Man U. fans everywhere. I was sharing something magical with millions of others across the world. But this surge of electricity, it's all about me. Me and Julie C. I watch her in her royal blue leotard and matching shorts and it's like she's there in a spotlight going through her routine just for me. Then this nagging thought comes knocking on my brain door. What about her personality? What if I pluck up the courage to talk to her and I don't like her. Think of it, she could be Miss Universe on the outside and the Wicked Witch of the East on the inside! A bit like the women on *Jerry Springer*. Oh no, don't tell me she's a bimbo. What if Julie's trailer trash?

'What's she like to talk to?'

Let her be nice, let her be nice, let her be nice.

'I like her.'

Yes!

'She's really friendly. She's dead popular already. I've never seen a new kid make friends so quickly.'

I press my nose against the window, my breath clouding the glass and almost obscuring my view of her doing a handstand, then gliding effortlessly into a perfect forward roll. Bobby brings me back to earth with a playful thump on the arm.

'Terry, I know you're head over heels in love and all that, but can we get to English? Spotty doesn't like you being late.'

He's right. Mr Spottiswood is the strictest teacher on the staff. Reluctantly, I start to detach myself from the window. That's when it happens. Julie pads to her Reebok sports bag and pulls out, of all things, a Liverpool shirt. I go through agonies as she slips it over her head. How can this be happening to me? Here I am watching the girl of my dreams and she's wearing the colours of our arch-enemies, the evil empire at the opposite end of the East Lancashire Road, Liverpool FC.

'Something wrong?' asks Bobby.

'Uh huh,' I tell him. 'Everything. She's only a Liverpool fan.'

Bobby shrugs.

'Never stopped me. I've been out with two Liverpudlians and I'm an Evertonian. I've even been out with one girl who didn't like football.'

We move along the corridor.

'Hurry up,' says Bobby. 'Your mind's still in the gym.'

He's right, it's up there hanging on the wall bars, transfixed by Julie Carter. Luckily, we beat Spotty to class. Just. That's when Bobby comes out with one of his famous useless facts:

'Do you know where the word gymnasium comes from?'

'No.'

'It's Greek. A place where you exercise naked.'

My mind falls off the wall bars. Bobby gives me a funny look.

'Terry, are you sweating?'

Sweating? It's a wonder I haven't had a heart attack!

Tuesday 20th June
3.10 p.m.

The build-up starts here. No homework tonight, I've cleared the decks so that I can watch every second of studio discussion, every instant of the live match action.

England v. Romania.

The last group match of Euro 2000. Win or draw and we're through to the quarter-finals to play Italy. Lose and it's just the latest in the line of Great English Disasters.

'That's all we've got to do,' I remind Bobby, as if he needs reminding. 'Avoid defeat and we're through.'

'Piece of cake,' says Bobby. 'Though the Azurri will be tougher.'

'I'm not so sure Romania will be that easy,' I say. 'They beat us in the World Cup, remember.'

'Only because of that plank Le Saux,' says Bobby. 'Petrescu did him for pace and strength. Can't trust a Southerner to get anything right.'

I smile. He's right. Whoever heard of a footballer from the Channel Islands? Phil Neville's a good Northern lad. He'll show him how it's done.

'Want to come round to ours to watch it?' I ask. 'You can have your tea first if you like.'

'Don't mind if I do,' says Bobby. 'I'll just phone Mum and let her know.'

So there's Bobby on his mobile and me waiting for him by the school gates when Julie walks past with Kelly Magee. Bobby says Kelly's the spitting image of Sabrina, the Teenage Witch, but I think he's exaggerating. In her bad moments she looks more like Salem, the cat. If you ask me, even in her best clothes and fully made up she doesn't register above seven on the cuteness scale. Bobby probably fancies her. Let's face it, he fancies just about anything in a skirt. Now Julie, she's a definite ten. She even looks good in her school uniform. I ask you, green blazer and tie, blue jumper and skirt and she still looks good.

I find myself staring at her sports bag. The Liverpool shirt is hanging out of the top. It's like a red rag to this particular bull. I mean, football is the lens through which I see the world.

'What're you staring at?' asks Kelly.

'N–nothing,' I stammer, caught in the act.

I look all round me, as if my eyes alighted on Julie for just one nanosecond, purely by chance.

'He was staring at you, Julie.'

There's no conning Kelly. She's been out with more boys than I've had bacon toasties and she knows all the tricks. She flounces by, her eyes raking me with invisible fire. Julie doesn't even give me a second look. She must be used to boys staring.

'Weirdo,' observes Kelly. 'Freak-a-zoid.'

Julie doesn't say a word.

'Made the first move already, have you?' says Bobby as he slips his mobile away. 'You dirty dog. Quick off the blocks this time, eh?'

'Let's go,' I say, ignoring him.

'Put your tongue back in,' says Bobby before coming out with one of his famous useless facts: 'Did you know that by the age of twelve months you've dribbled one hundred and forty five litres of saliva?'

He looks at Julie. 'Mind you, anybody would find Julie Carter mouth-watering.'

I look away. I know I've gone bright red, the colour of that stinking Liverpool shirt.

Tuesday 20th June
7.30 p.m.

Something's up. There's definitely an atmosphere. Bobby's noticed it too. While we were having our tea, Dad said something under his breath to Mum about having a house meeting soon.

House meeting?

What's that about? We're not *Guardian* readers. We don't have house meetings. Who does he think we are, characters in some divvy sit-com? Ever since he mentioned the house meeting Mum has been stamping round slamming cupboards and plonking down cups. For a while I thought it was this new cabbage diet she's been on, but it's more than that. She isn't a happy bunny.

'Should I go?' Bobby asks just before kick-off.

Even somebody as thick-skinned as our Mr Bubbly is feeling uncomfortable.

'Don't be daft,' I tell him. 'It'll blow over. It always does. Besides, you'd miss the action.'

'So who's going to be the match-winner?' asks Dad, flopping into his armchair with a bottle of Stella. He's wearing the United away strip for the game so it's obvious what he expects to hear.

'Beckham,' says Bobby, 'Everything comes from his crosses.'

'Scholes,' I say. 'Watch his runs from deep.'

But it isn't either of the United players who catch the eye early on. Or even an Englishman. The Romanians are playing a fluent game of pass and move and within two minutes Ilie cracks a free kick round the wall. Nigel Martyn does well to stop Moldovan's shot. Bobby, Dad and I exchange worried looks. It isn't going according to plan. Twenty-two minutes into the match things are going from bad to worse. Chivu tries a chipped cross and it clears Martyn and bounces in off the upright.

We're 1–0 down.

'Not again,' groans Dad. 'They're going to throw it away as usual.'

Bobby gives me a meaningful look.

'Why are Dads always so negative?' he whispers.

'It's genetic,' I whisper back. 'They've got a whinging gene.'

'We'll get back into it, Mr Payne,' says Bobby.

He's right. Five minutes before the interval Paul Ince is brought down in the box.

'Ex-Man U,' I point out proudly. I conveniently forget that he's also ex-Liverpool.

Shearer sends the keeper the wrong way and me and Bobby are skidding across the wooden floor on our knees, arms raised in celebration. Then, in first-half injury time, a touch from Ince followed by the deftest of flicks from Paul Scholes puts Michael Owen through.

He uses his pace to get clear of the advancing keeper and slots the ball into the net. It doesn't get any better than this. 'Told you Scholes would do it,' I yell, bouncing up and down on the couch.

'Owen was the one who scored, you know,' Bobby points out.

'The hard work was already done by then,' says Dad.

He never was one to give a Liverpool player credit if he could help it. I wonder what Julie would make of the scene.

During the half-time break we're eating Kit-Kats. Mum's sadly munching an apple. She's sworn off chocolate. Something to do with the size of her love handles. We keep reading the scoreline. We can hardly believe our luck.

'Romania have played us off the park,' says Dad, 'And we're 2–1 up.'

'Just got to hold on to it now,' says Bobby. 'We were two up against Portugal and we still lost.'

'Not this time,' says Dad. 'You're going to see the old bulldog spirit come through.'

But there isn't much bulldog spirit on show after the break. The game has hardly restarted when Martyn punches the ball out to Munteanu. The Romanian chests it down and volleys it into the net. It's 2–2 and we're gutted. It doesn't get any worse than this.

'See how Martyn flapped at that?' says Bobby.

'Typical Leeds player,' snorts Dad, a bit unfairly I reckon.

'How much longer's this on?' moans Amy, my little sister, as she puts in an appearance in her Mulan nightie, the one she got in Florida.

'Ages,' I tell her, waving her out of the way of the screen.

For the rest of the match we're on the edge of our seats.

Romania are pressing forward all the time. Their passing is neater and crisper than ours. But if we can only hold on...

We're defending too deep,' says Dad. 'We're asking for it.' And we get it.

'Two minutes left,' says Dad. 'Just two minutes. Come on, lads. Dig in.'

'Come on,' I say.

'Come on,' Bobby echoes desperately.

Somehow we all know what's coming. It's like destiny. A locomotive called defeat. But with the seconds ticking away we start to hope.

'Blow, ref,' pleads Dad.

Then the sky caves in. Moldovan drives into the penalty box. Phil Neville is challenging him all the way. Then the ex-Coventry man is past Phil on the outside.

'Stick to him,' I yell.

'But don't bring him...'

Phil lunges and flattens Moldovan.

'...down,' groans Bobby.

'He dived,' I cry, jumping to my feet in outrage as the ref points to the spot. 'Blatant dive. That Moldovan was the same when he played in the Premiership. Phil got a definite touch on the ball.'

Dad shakes his head. 'Not this time, Terry. The ref's got it right. It's a penalty.'

I remember Euro 96. Not penalties again. Not this.

Bobby covers his face with a cushion.

'I can't look,' he says.

I look and I wish I hadn't. Ganea converts from the spot. Agonising moments later it's full time. England 2, Romania 3.

I'm hollow, like somebody's shoved a pipe down my throat and hoovered out my insides. 'It's David Beckham all over again,' says Dad. 'The Man U-haters will be lining up to have a go.'

I remember the way Beckham kicked out in the World Cup game against Argentina and wince. Opposition fans booed Beckham for two years because of his red card. United were hated even more than usual. I took a lot of stick for Becks' rush of blood.

'Phil Neville's going to pay for that blunder.'

I think of all the anti-United feeling at school and Julie in her Liverpool shirt. Phil Neville isn't the only one who's going to suffer.

Tuesday 20th June
10.20 p.m.

Bobby's gone home and Amy's tucked up in bed, so it's just me, Mum and Dad. We've been raking over the ashes of defeat for half an hour now, getting more and more down in the dumps. Even Mum, who doesn't have much of an interest in the beautiful game, is affected by it. The post-mortem is even more painful than usual after an England failure. Dad's ranting about Kevin Keegan like it's personal, and he's taking Phil Neville's mistake really badly, going on about how he's never going to be able to hold his head up at work.

'All those Scousers just waiting to take a rise out of me.'

After a while I start to wonder whether all this hot air really is about football. It's as if football's just the excuse, something to hang his rage on. Something's scratching away at the back of my mind, something about…yes, a house meeting.

'What's this house meeting anyway?' I ask, never dreaming I'm opening up a can of giant worms.

'Not now, eh, Geoff?' says Mum, a pleading look in her eyes. 'Surely it can wait until you're in a better mood.'

'Better mood,' snaps Dad. 'That's a good one.'

I'm starting to get worried. They've never been much for arguments, my parents. They usually show all the passion of a deep-frozen cod. But tonight I can almost touch the suppressed rage crackling between them.

'May as well know now as later,' grunts Dad. 'The lad's fifteen. It's not like anything's going to change. We'd just be putting it off.'

He's got this wild look in his eyes as though he wants to hurt everybody, especially himself. All of a sudden I'm not just worried, I'm scared.

'Geoff,' said Mum, panicky and anxious, 'don't say something you'll regret.'

But the wildness has got hold of Dad. He's in full flow.

'England throw it away again…lousy job…dead end life… all I do is work and what do I get for it? No thanks…feel like chucking it.'

'Dad, what are you on about?'

'Shall I tell him what I'm on about, Sharon?' he demands, eyes wilder than ever.

That seals it. This isn't about England. Even thirty years of hurt couldn't get him in this state. No, it's something else. I can feel the earth slipping away from under my feet.

'I'm moving out Terry, that's what I'm on about. I'm getting my own place.'

That can of worms, the creatures are all the size of anacondas with teeth like vampires.

'Geoff!' cries Mum. 'Not like this.'

The giant worms are chewing through my heart, ventricle by shredded ventricle.

'We've talked about how we'd tell the children.'

I can just imagine it. I've read about it in Mum's magazines when I was hunting for the naughty bits on the agony aunt pages: *It's your partner you're splitting up from, not your children.*

Well, wrong. I know exactly who Dad's splitting up from. All of us. I've read the little guides. *How to explain it to the kids. Letting them down gently.*

Well, believe me, there's nothing gentle about the way Dad's let me down. I feel like I've been run over by a lorry. This has come right out of the blue. Where were the quarrels, the raised voices, the thrown crockery, the slammed doors? Dad, where were the warnings?

'We've been drifting apart for a while,' says Mum, trying to salvage something after the explosion. 'It's not your fault, Terry.'

Not my fault. Well, duh! I *know* it's not my fault. It's yours, you pair of lousy fakes, pretending to be a couple when all the while you were planning to chuck your marriage in the bin.

'How long have you known?' I ask. 'How long have you had this planned?'

'A couple of weeks,' says Dad. 'Well, a month or two actually.'

The bombshell explodes in my head. This has been going on since Easter at least.

'A month or two!'

All the things we've done in that time flash through my mind. Parents' evening, they were both at that. Mr and Mrs Supportive. The day out at Alton Towers. Swimming at Heatwaves. Amy's birthday party. I see it all in freeze-frame. Me and Amy grinning our stupid heads off and all the time our family was a big, fat, lousy lie. Happy families, happy rotten families.

'I'm going to bed,' I say, making for the door.

I don't even want to look at them.

'No, Terry, not like this,' says Mum. 'Sit down for a couple of minutes.'

'Why?' I ask. 'Is Dad going to change his mind?'

Dad shakes his head. He's got this weird look on his face, like the guy who's let the evil genie out of the bottle and can't find the cork.

'Then I'm going to bed.'

Tuesday 20th June
11.30 p.m.

Today's a day I won't forget in a hurry.

When I saw Julie in the gym it was like conquering Everest. The feeling I had, it was like I just couldn't get any higher. But there's something they don't tell you about getting to the top of the mountain. From then on, the only way is down.

And boy, did I choose the quickest way to descend! The key moments flash through my mind as I fall.

Nigel Martyn flapping that cross...

...punching the ball to Munteanu...

...Phil Neville bringing down Moldovan

...Alan Shearer crying.

The air is rushing more quickly. More moments:

...Dad ranting and waving at the TV...

...Mum with her pleading eyes...

...Dad saying it's over.

20th June 2000: the best of days, the worst of days.

● ● ● ●

2

Wednesday 21st June
8.50 a.m.

To understand how I'm feeling as I trudge towards the school gates, you'll need to know something about Knowsley Manor High. The school is in Prescot on the eastern edge of Liverpool. The town is at the top of a long hill. At the bottom of the hill is Huyton where most of the kids come from. So what does that mean? I'll tell you what it means. Man U. fans are outnumbered about ten to one by Liverpudlians and Evertonians. We get more stick than a dog in the park. I missed Bobby this morning so into the valley of death trudged the one.

Here's what I hear as I reach the gates:

'I hear some plank of a Man U. player's sunk England again.'

The voice belongs to Fitz. That's John Fitzpatrick, my captain in the Year 10 football team. He's cock of the school. Bright, sporty, good with the girls. He seems to have been out with most of them. I've spent the last four years here trying to be just like him.

'What is it with you Mancs? First Beckham sabotages the World Cup for us, now Neville loses us Euro 2000.'

I'm trying to shrug it off. Dad was gone when I got up this morning and I'm in no mood for this. I'm all hot and red and my skin's prickling all over. Fitz knows he's getting to me.

'It wasn't Phil Neville's fault,' I retort.

'So whose was it?' asks Fitz with a mocking laugh. 'How did Romania get that penalty then, an act of God?'

I'm really starting to dislike Fitz. He's gone from role model to arch-enemy in ninety seconds.

What was I doing copying this Dingus Malingus?

'Martyn was to blame for the first two goals,' I say. 'And Paul Scholes set up Owen's goal, remember.'

I'm taking it too seriously. Why can't I just ignore him, let it roll over me the way Bobby does? I'll tell you why, Julie has put in an appearance and she's watching our argument with interest.

'Hey, Kelly, Julie,' says Fitz, 'Have you heard this one? He says it wasn't Neville's fault last night.'

'So whose fault was it?' asks Kelly Magee.

All these Scousers seem to be reading from a prepared script. I look into her Sabrina lookalike blue eyes and want to tell her where to get off. But she's Julie's new best mate so I keep my lip buttoned.

'He was unlucky,' I tell her.

'Unlucky! Is that what you call it?'

The three of them are laughing. At me. I can't stand to look at them, especially Julie. Why does she have to join in? But why shouldn't she? They're in the top maths set together and they all support Liverpool. I'm the odd one out here.

'Look at the state of him,' says John. 'I think he's going to cry.'

'Don't be stupid,' I retort. 'I didn't see any of your wonderful Liverpool players doing much either.'

'In case you didn't notice,' Julie says. 'Michael Owen scored.'

She says it matter-of-factly. There's no venom in her words. 'He took it brilliantly.'

'And he's gorgeous,' adds Kelly, sticking her unwanted oar in.

'Yes,' says Julie, acting all swoony. 'Definitely gorgeous.'

I look at her for the first time and suddenly I'm melting in those dark brown eyes. I like her and she likes Michael Owen. The eternal triangle.

'Yes,' I admit grudgingly. 'He took the goal well.'

'Now that's a first,' says Kelly. 'A Manc who admits he's wrong.'

'Bit like a Scouser who keeps her opinions to herself,' I snap back.

Me and my big mouth. I see Julie's heart-stopping eyes narrowing. Congratulations Terry, you've just forced her even closer to the dreaded Fitz. Make a mental note: the girl you're mad about is a Scouser too. Now she's in a nark with you. What have I done? Quick, backtrack.

'I didn't mean all Scousers,' I stammer. 'I meant...'

'You don't know what you mean,' says Fitz, twisting the knife. 'Typical Manc. Anyway, I've got something for you.'

He's rummaging in his bag,

'It's here somewhere. I cut it out specially for you. Yes, here it is.' With a flourish, he produces a cutting from the *Mirror*. The headline pierces my heart. It consists of just one word: ROMANIAC!

'Wonder what United have got planned for the next World Cup,' Fitz muses. 'A Gary Neville own goal? You know, keep disaster in the family.'

With that they turn their backs and walk away. Not that I care about Fitz and Kelly. But the third back belongs to Julie and that hurts.

Wednesday 21st June
10.00 a.m.

Over half-way through double French and still no sign of Bobby. I decide to send him a text message: *Bobby, where are you? Terry.* The message comes back a couple of minutes later:

What do you mean, where am I? Where are you?

Which sets off a hi-tech, low-sense exchange:

Me: *I'm in school, where do you think?*

Bobby: *School! What time is it?*

Me: *Ten o'clock, you dope.*

Bobby: *Ten o'clock! Ohmigod. Mum didn't get me up.*

Me: *You're lucky.*

Bobby: *Come again?*

Me: *My mum and dad have just split up.*

Bobby: *I'm in a rush. Give me the gory details when I get in.*

Get your skates on, Bobby lad. I think of Fitz and all the other Liverpudlians dying to take a pop at me. Something tells me I'll need all the friends I've got for morning break.

Wednesday 21st June
10.30 a.m.

'Robert Quinn,' says Mrs Massie as he bursts through the door. 'What time do you call this?'

'Dix heures et demi,' Bobby answers in his best schoolboy French.

Mrs Massie doesn't see the joke.

'Have you been to the office to tell them you're in?'

'Yes.'

'And what cock and bull story did you give them?'

I can see Bobby biting his tongue. I know exactly what he'd say if he didn't stop himself: *Same cock and bull story I'm giving you.*

That's one of Bobby's problems. He always has to have the last word. Even if it's the wrong word. I've lost track of the times he's opened his mouth and put his size nine right in it.

'My asthma was bad, Miss. Did you know that by the age of twenty-one I will have breathed in enough air to inflate three-and-a-half million balloons?'

'Mm,' says Mrs Massie dryly. 'And by the end of this lesson you will have breathed out enough hot air to fill the Goodyear airship.'

Our appreciative ripple of laughter is interrupted only by the bell for mid-morning break. As we elbow our way down the corridor Bobby gives me a sideways look.

'So what's with the Payne family this fine and sunny day?'

'Dad's gone.'

'Gone where exactly?'

'Dunno.'

'How come?'

I open my mouth to answer. Mum's got it into her head that it's because she's put on a bit of weight. If she could only squeeze into a size 12 she'd still have a marriage. Somehow, I don't think that's it. But that's when I realise, *I don't know. I* don't know why he's gone, or even where he's gone.

'He's just gone.'

'I didn't know your folks were having problems.'

'That's just it, Bobby, neither did I.'

We spill out of the side door and made for the far side of the yard overlooking the sports hall. I think briefly of Julie in a blue leotard, permit myself a dreamy smile, then glance at Bobby.

'He came out with it after the match. I think the Romania fiasco set him off.'

'First time I've heard of a footy divorce,' says Bobby.

I do my best to sound off-hand about it, but I don't think Bobby's fooled. He can see how cut up I am.

'No, I mean it's been building up and the match was the last straw. He said all sorts of weird stuff.'

'Like what?'

'I dunno. Like he hates his job.'

'Double-glazing fitter. Don't think I'd fancy it either. They're always knocking on our front door. Nobody wants it.'

'Plenty of people have got it. Come to think of it, you have.'

I realise we've got off the subject. Any time now Bobby will furnish me with a number of depressed double-glazing fitters in the greater Merseyside region.

'It isn't right, Bobby. It came right out of the blue.'

'Sounds like my first divorce,' says Bobby.

Of course, I'd clean forgotten. His mum has been married twice, first to the baldy chap from St Helens – Bobby's dad – then to the man with the squint and the budgie from West Kirby. Funny taste in men, Bobby's mum. At the moment she's going out with this bloke from round the corner. Big guy with a cocker spaniel. Long furry ears and a shiny nose. The spaniel, not the boyfriend.

'You didn't expect it, then?'

'No way, I was thunderstruck. That wasn't the worst thing though.'

Right now, I can't imagine anything worse than the split.

'So what was?'

Bobby taps his nose knowingly.

'Access days, Terry. Access days.'

'Go on.'

'Your dad comes round to take you out. You must have seen them in McDonalds, miserable-looking men with their sprogs shovelling chips and chicken nuggets. At weekends they take up half the tables. I call it Access Alley.'

I've got the picture firmly fixed in my mind. Access Alley: lose hope all ye who enter here.

'Oh.'

'Oh is right Terry lad. I mean, your bedroom can only take so many beanie babies and plastic Disney characters. They take you everywhere at first, Camelot, Blue Planet Aquarium, Chester Zoo, the cinema. It's the guilt, you see, quickest route to their pockets. Then they get their first post-separation bank statement. After a while it's take-away pizza and a walk in Taylor Park. But that's not the worst of it.'

'No?'

'Oh no. On the rainy days it's back to Dad's bedsit with a video of *The Little Vampire* and a KFC.'

He looks around furtively. He's enjoying this, initiating me into the terrors of marital meltdown.

'But you've still not hit rock bottom. You know what comes next?'

I hardly dare ask.

'No.'

'One day, one dreadful day your dad will turn round and ask: *So what do you want to do today? He's* all out of ideas. Either that, or he's just stopped caring. That's when you know your relationship has gone critical.'

'Oh, behave, Bobby,' I say.

'I'm not kidding,' he says. 'You know all that father-son bonding stuff? Forget it. I hardly see my old man now. Better that way, I suppose.'

I can tell by the look on his face he doesn't really mean it. There's a space in his heart that will forever be occupied by a baldy guy from St Helens.

'I know my dad, Bobby. He took me to the Champions League Final in Barcelona, remember. You don't do that if you don't care. It was the greatest day of my life. And we shared it. Me and my dad.'

The greatest day of my life. Rivalled only by the sight of Julie Carter in the sports hall.

'We go to Old Trafford together for every home game. It's the highlight of my week. None of that Access Alley stuff is ever going to happen to us.'

I can see the future stretching out before me, one long Sir Matt Busby Way, straight and true. The only difference is, Mum and Dad are on opposite pavements.

Bobby shakes his head slowly.

'You can't rely on anything once your parents separate. Things are going to change, Terry. They're going to change a lot.'

I can see Dad and myself walking down the Ramblas singing *Championes* and reliving Sheringham and Solskjaer's goals all the way back home to Prescot. Us end up as two sad lads eating chicken pieces in a bedsit?

Never.

Wednesday 21st June
1.15 p.m.

We're getting changed for football when Bobby drops his bombshell.

'You've got a rival for the lovely Julie's affections,' he tells me.

'Who?'

'Fitz.'

I look across at John Fitzpatrick. I thought he'd been hanging round her a lot.

'You know I was wondering how Julie got so popular in such a short space of time?' says Bobby.

'Uh huh.'

It's hard to reply properly with a lump in your throat.

'Well, it turns out she knew loads of the kids here even before she came to Knowsley Manor. They met at the gym club at the leisure centre.'

'Who did?'

'Julie, Kelly, Pepsey Cooper, Fitz.

'Hang on a minute. Fitz does gymnastics?'

'No, you dope. His little sister does. It turns out old Fitzy's known Julie for the last six months, ever since his Hayley joined the gym club at the leisure centre. If you're going to make a move, you'd better do it sharpish. You know Fitz's reputation.'

159

Do I? Fitz has had loads of girlfriends. I mean, we're talking two figures. That's why they call him, Frisky Fitzy. Some say he's got a bit of a look of Michael Owen, which helps. Oh great, it'll really help with Julie. She's *mad* about Michael Owen. That love triangle's turned into a love quadrilateral. Bobby's about to go when something occurs to me.

'What *did* happen to you this morning?'

'You're not going to believe this,' says Bobby.

'Try me.'

'Mum thought I was staying at yours last night. She didn't see me come in. Too busy with lover boy.'

(That's the one with the spaniel.)

'So when she went out to work this morning she locked the house up. Only locked me inside, didn't she?'

Bobby's front door is a double-glazed unit with seven mortice locks. My dad fitted it cheap.

'So what did you do?'

'I couldn't find my keys. I only had to climb out of my bedroom window and shin down the drainpipe. Got some really funny looks from the neighbours.'

'Bobby,' I say, 'It could only happen to you.'

He shrugs in that *stuff happens* way of his.

'Anyway,' says Bobby, 'I've got to pee. See you out there.'

I watch Fitz lacing up his boots and suddenly I'm wondering where you can buy voodoo dolls with Michael Owen haircuts.

'Something the matter?' he asks, catching my eye.

'No, why?'

'Dunno, just thought you might want to apologise for Chopper Neville's act of madness.'

'Oh, let it drop.'

Fitz starts to clatter across the tiled floor on his new studs. I admire the boots but not the boy in them.

'What, and let a Manc off the hook? Never.'

I'm last out of the changing rooms. As I go to pull on my shirt I catch my reflection in the mirror. Milk-bottle skin, freckles, bony shoulders, untidy ginger hair and legs like matchsticks. I have this recurring nightmare. I'm growing up to look like Chris Evans.

'Hey, carrot top,' shouts Fitz. 'We're waiting for you.'

I bite my lip. Julie and Fitz. No, not that. Anything but that.

Wednesday 21st June
1.45 p.m.

Fitz is laughing at me. He's done me twice for pace and his team is 2–0 up already. I've got a great football brain. It's the body that's the problem.

This was my last chance to impress Mr Shooter and get myself into the side for the Knowsley Boys' Cup Final. We're playing Blackridge on Monday after school. It's me or Chris Lawlor for the last midfield place.

'You'd better buck your ideas up,' says Bobby. 'Six Guns has got Chris pencilled in for Monday.'

Mr Shooter is making notes on the touch-line.

'I know. Fitz is doing this on purpose.'

'Then don't let him. Get tighter on him.'

Six Guns walks purposefully to the centre and gestures to the teams.

'Second half, lads. Ready?'

Fitz is doing hamstring stretches on the edge of the centre circle. Suddenly I'm seeing him in a new light. He isn't just into girls any more. He's into *my* girl. He really loves himself. I reckon lads like him must come in flat-packs. Construct-a-Creep.

'Psst,' hisses Bobby. 'Seen who's watching? They must have a free period.'

It's Kelly and Julie. That settles it. I'll get tight on Fitz all right. He isn't going to make a monkey out of me a third time. Jamie Sneddon picks up the ball and looks for Fitz. He's coming my way with his right arm raised.

I decide to close him down and get to the ball first, putting it into touch.

'More like it,' says Bobby.

I permit myself a smile. I hope Julie was watching. Ten minutes later Gary Tudor turns provider. Again I get in before Fitz, clearing the ball downfield. Paul Scully gets on to the end of it and pulls one back for us. 2–1 down. Now *we* can make a game of it. I can see Six Guns making notes. I'm not doing myself any harm at all. I wonder what Julie thinks. No, don't let your mind wander. Just stay focused, Terry lad.

No Phil Nevilles.

Five minutes from the end Paul gets on the wrong side of his defender and scores with a glancing header. We've pulled level, 2–2.

'No silly mistakes,' says Bobby, clapping his hands. 'Keep it tight lads.'

It's easier said than done. Fitz's team are pressing us back. I glance at my watch. Two minutes left. Just like last night. Keep your concentration, Terry lad.

No Phil Nevilles.

Then I hear Bobby screaming at me. Gary Tudor has played a long ball over the top and put Fitz clear. I scamper across to intercept the ball. He's in the penalty box. God, he's fast. Just like Michael Owen, low centre of gravity and lots of pace. He's weaving and doing step-overs as I go to meet him, then he pushes it ahead of him, trying to turn me. I'm dying to get a foot in. My every instinct is screaming *flatten him. Demolish the Knowsley Manor Casanova.*

But no, I can't do it.

No Phil Nevilles.

We're shoulder to shoulder. I'm determined to force him wide. That's when he taps the ball through my legs. The lousy rat's nutmegged me!

I try to get out of his way, but his pace takes him into me. We go down in a tangle of legs and arms. Fitz is up first, arms raised. I scramble up after him waving mine.

'No pen,' I cry. 'Accidental. He ran into me.'

But Six Guns is having none of it. He points straight to the spot. Penalty. Fitz walks up and strokes the ball in. I look over to the touchline. Kelly and Julie are clapping wildly. The next ninety seconds fly past. It's too late to equalise again. I look from Julie on the touchline to Six Guns making his notes. No way am I in the team.

I'm out of luck with both of them.

Double Thirteen
Eleanor Updale

THURSDAY 12TH FEBRUARY: 10.30PM

I know I promised myself I wouldn't start this diary till
tomorrow. To mark the New Year. Not for everyone, of
course. Just for me, and a few other poor souls who will be
having their birthdays on Friday 13th. The unluckiest day of the
year. I worked it out on the computer at school. It's actually
quite rare. There are only two Friday 13ths this year. No year
has more than three. Because of leap years you can go for
ages without having your birthday on a Friday. It's not quite
as unlikely as winning the lottery, but you probably only get
about a dozen birthday Fridays in a lifetime. And I get one of
mine tomorrow. That's in an hour and a half from now. I'll be
thirteen years old on Friday 13th February. Double Thirteen.
Double Unlucky.

It's a big thing, Thirteen. A teenager. Mum's already started
joking about it. She was deliberately winding me up tonight. All
I did was chuck my pudding in the bin when Chloe said it was
loaded with calories.

'Oooh Oooh' said Mum, in that sing-song voice parents know
will really hit you, 'Oooh Oooh. Teenage angst!'

Well, of course I couldn't help stomping off and slamming
the door after that. And they thought I'd gone. They thought
I couldn't hear them laughing about me in the kitchen.

'Oh God,' said Chloe. 'Is that what it's going to be like after
tomorrow? Seven years of flouncing around.'

I mean, what does she know about it? She's only eight. She's naturally skinny, like I was then. She doesn't know how it hurts. I know I'm fat. I can feel it all jiggling when I walk. That's why I don't run. It bounces then, and I can tell everyone's laughing at me. Even the ones who say I'm normal. But that's because they're looking at things like my horrible fingers – they're like knobbly sticks. Or my neck – you can see the bones in my shoulders. Disgusting. But you can't see my ribs. Not unless I breathe in. And not through a T-shirt.

I didn't want them to know I'd been listening outside the kitchen, so I came upstairs and had a bath before bed. But I was starving afterwards, and I couldn't get to sleep. So I went down and got myself some food. Some jelly and a dollop of chocolate mousse, with some of that spray cream on top. And that's why I'm writing this diary. I realised as soon as I got up here what I was doing. I've read about it. It's bulimia, isn't it? Bingeing. All part of the teenage thing. It's starting already. I've got to resist it. The bowl's on the floor here by the bed, and I'm not going to touch it. I'm not even going to look at it. I'm going to ignore it. So I've started this diary early to take my mind off food. To make a note that thirteen's come a few hours too soon. I'll try to write every day. To say what it's really like being thirteen. Then, if I have a daughter, I'll read it and remind myself. And I won't crack stupid insensitive jokes that only get people angry and lead them to do things that make them seem like typical teenagers, when they're not.

And anyway, this is going to be a big year for me. I'm not just going to be a thirteen-year-old. I'll be a thirteen-year-old whose birthday was on Friday 13th. I mean, I haven't got a hope.

I can see what it's going to be like. I've watched the others at school. I copy them. I mean, there are some things you have to live up to. You don't want to be a dork. People like Mum laugh about teenagers, but what they don't understand is that we don't have any choice. Does Mum want me to be a joke? I've got to do what the others do. I've got to be the same. Even though I'm different. Especially because I'm different.

I'm unlucky.

So maybe everyone at school is going to hate me anyway. Like they hate that boy in Year Nine with the violin. I mean, he practises *at lunchtime*. In one of those padded rooms on the music corridor. And his mum drives him everywhere. She parks right outside on the zig-zags. And she kisses him. There. In the street. Right in front of everyone. And at the Christmas concert she talked to the teachers loads. She called Mr Newman 'Colin'. Right there, where everyone could hear. And she let him tap her on the arm. We all saw it.

We were stacked up, balanced on chairs and blocks on the stage, waiting to sing that stupid medley of *Disney* songs. Well, I say sing, but of course I just mime. Mr Newman doesn't know. I'm better at miming than half the pop stars you see on TV. The violin boy and people like him sing. It's so embarrassing. At least I managed not to tell my mum about the concert until it was too late for her to change her shifts at work, so she couldn't come. I didn't have to worry about her showing me up by waving or something like that. But it was still a nightmare. I mean, *Disney* songs. What do they think we are? Children? They have no idea. Even if they realised our maturity, they'd just make it worse. Make us sing old pop songs or something. Like Year Ten at that concert. I mean, kids singing *Yesterday!* Even the botox-faced bloke who wrote it would realise how naff it is, sung by a school choir, sounding their 't's and rolling their 'r's. But Mr

Newman was grinning like an idiot, thinking he was being cool or something. You can guess what he must have been like when he was at school. He'll have been like the violin boy. I bet his mum waved at concerts. Probably still does. Probably buys his clothes as well. And now there's her precious Colin, grown-up, and still a nerd, grinning and giggling like he's some sort of rebel for playing ancient pop songs in a school. It was embarrassing enough to *watch* Year Ten doing it. Imagine what it was like to be up on the stage. Child abuse.

So that's how bad things are now. That's life before Double Thirteen. It's that grim already, even without the teenage label and the bad luck I'll be getting from tomorrow. And I can imagine what that's going to be like. Here's a typical day in my new life. I'm going to write about how I think it will go. And by the way, writing this diary is working. I haven't touched the food in the bowl. So...

A DAY IN THE FUTURE: IN THE YEAR OF DOUBLE THIRTEEN

I get up. I've overslept because the crappy alarm clock Chloe gave me for Christmas has dead batteries. I mean, why doesn't Mum ever remember to buy batteries? It's not that hard. Anyway I hate that clock. It's got a picture of *BOIZNOYZE* on the face. The hands join on right over Jamie's nose. I think Chloe got it just to take the mickey. She knew I liked Jamie best – though the truth is I was already going off them, and I wasn't surprised when they broke up in January, after the row with their manager and that really terrible single that only got to number 31.

So, anyway, I'm already late, and I forget my geography homework (which I've actually *done* by the way, though Mrs

Drysdale doesn't believe me, and puts me down for a detention to do it again on paper, which I'll have to stick into my book, so completely obliterating the evidence that I've had to do it twice). Because I'm late, I've missed the bus my friends get, and I'm stuck with a load of dorks, and I have to walk in the school gates with them. And Robbie, this gorgeous boy in Year Nine, sees me going in with them and thinks I'm their friend. And it gets worse, because the teacher gives me a Duty for being late, and it's handing out hymn books at assembly, and now Robbie thinks I'm some sort of God-Squadder too, so I know I'm finished there. And I'm sitting in Prayers just telling Jessica all this when the Head sees me talking, and makes me *stand up* in front of everyone and say what I was talking about. And I can't think what to say. So he gets all facetious and says (in that voice they use when they want to make you look really stupid), 'Perhaps you were commenting on the passage I was reading. What was it about?'

Of course I wasn't listening, so I think it's probably the usual stuff about God is Love, so I take a chance and say, 'Love, Sir.'

And everybody laughs. And I know I've picked the worst word I could have said, because the Head is into it now, and stays sarcastic, and says, 'You can discuss your love life in the playground! But not today. Today, you can sit outside my room in silence at break.' And he doesn't say it, but I know he's thinking, *'While everyone else talks about you in the yard. And they all think you fancy one of those dorks you were with this morning.'* And I won't be there to tell them all they're wrong now, and it's that stupid alarm clock with *BOIZNOYZE* on that's to blame. And maybe I say that out loud by mistake, and someone hears and tells everyone that I still like *BOIZNOYZE,* even though I don't any more, and never really did anyway. And all morning people are humming that tune and doing the stupid hand movements from the video. And someone says how I know all the moves. And it's true I did learn them, but I only did them for a joke, and now they're making it sound as if I really liked *BOIZNOYZE,* and still do, even though everyone knows they're rubbish. And my bad luck continues, because Robbie from Year Nine is passing while this is going on and hears it all and gives me a patronising smirk. So I lash out at one of the girls who's laughing and, more bad luck, Mr Corley comes round the corner just as I accidentally catch her cheek with my ring (which I'm not supposed to be wearing, and wouldn't be, if I'd had time to remember to take it off when I was rushing to school this morning) and I'm marched back to the Head's office where he gives me a Very Serious Talk and makes me late for lunch, so I have to sit with the geeks who take in packed lunches, and I'm right next to the violin boy, who's actually got *home-made wholemeal sandwiches,* and I just want to die, because people will think I'm there on purpose, and that I fancy him.

So I'm finished anyway, but my bad luck gets even worse, and my period starts in Double Maths, and I don't realise until I hear people laughing behind me at when I stand up at the end of the lesson and there's a red patch on my dress. And they send me to the nurse, who goes all understanding, which is the worst thing of all, and she lends me a spare pair of school tracksuit trousers to wear home, so even people who don't know me, and haven't had the chance to get to hate me yet, think I like sport and that I'm in some kind of *team* or something, and so I'm finished with them too, and I haven't even got home to all the bad luck that waits for me there.

THURSDAY 12TH FEBRUARY: 11.15PM

So that's what it's going to be like for me in the year of Double Thirteen. But there's something else I've worked out. I'm going to get one extra bit of bad luck right at the end. This year is a leap year, right, so instead of my next two birthdays being at the weekend (so I can enjoy them at home, and don't have to go to school), guess what? The extra leap-year day pushes my fourteenth birthday to a Sunday. When I'm fifteen, it will be a Monday. A cold, winter, school Monday. It isn't fair.

Do you think the bad luck will stop a year from tonight, as I turn fourteen on that ordinary Sunday? Well, even if it does, I've got news for you. You know I said I'd checked out the calendar on the computer? Well guess when my next Friday 13th comes round? On my *eighteenth* birthday. So I'll enter adulthood unlucky. But it's worse than that. I know when I'm going to die. The day I'm eighty. It's too much of a coincidence. All my big dates are unlucky days. Thirteen, eighteen, eighty. It's meant to be. Somebody up there doesn't like me.

I'd better get some sleep.

11.25PM

No such luck. I'm still here. Still thinking about tomorrow. About the bad luck. Perhaps it has already started. I'll be so tired tomorrow I won't be able to do anything right, and everyone will hate me. I read in a magazine how your skin goes all grey and floppy if you don't get enough rest. Your eyeballs go dull. Maybe I'll get little red veins in them like Mrs McMichael, the one with the triplets. She told me she hasn't had a full night's sleep in two years. I saw her bending over the pushchair the other day. Her hair's gone all thin on top.

So I'll be tired and ugly.

And bald.

I'm turning off the light.

11.30PM

I'm still here. It said in the same magazine that if you write down the time every five minutes, the effort of trying to stay awake actually sends you to sleep. And when you wake up in the morning you can look at your notes and see exactly when you dropped off. Apparently insomniacs get more sleep than they think. They're just too tired to work it out or something.

So, it's 11.32 now. I'll be back at 11.37.

11.37PM

Still awake.

11.42PM

No luck yet.

11.50PM

Must have got a couple of minutes' shuteye somewhere there! But here I am, back again, and it's nearly midnight. Might as well stay awake now to see my birthday in. I'll just go to the loo, then come back to bed and wait to see what bad luck the Fates have in store for me. What's the bet that the ceiling falls in at one minute past twelve?

FRIDAY 13TH FEBRUARY: 7PM

Well, I didn't have to wait for 12.01. Didn't even have to wait for Friday 13th to get officially started, as it turned out. Remember that dish of jelly and chocolate mousse on the floor? I didn't. Put my foot straight in it. Fell over and broke my ankle. Agony. But Casualty is quicker in the middle of the night. Remember that if you're ever planning an accident.

They all had a good laugh when they saw m·· date of b..ih.

'13 on Friday 13th!' said the doctor. 'I'm not superstitious, but you haven't wasted much time prov ng me wrong!'

Mum was nice though, considering there was jelly, chocolate, and cream all over the carpet, and she had to drive me to hospital in the middle of the night. And they let me choose the colour of my plaster cast. It's blue. Really cool. We dropped in at school this morning and everyone crowded round, and signed it with felt tips. I've got crutches too. Some of the girls looked at me with real envy. I've never had that before. It was great.

When Dad got home this evening the family gave me my presents. Chloe got me a new alarm clock. It's very designer. Stark chrome. Not a pop group in sight. No embarrassment. Batteries included. And I'm writing this on my new laptop. I've copied in all the stuff I wrote in my notebook last night, and now I'll finish off and put in a DVD. I'll be able to watch films in bed, with my foot up on a pillow. Mum's getting me a hot chocolate and the last slice of birthday cake. Even Chloe's being really friendly and helpful.

When the plaster comes off I'll have to go to physio every Wednesday afternoon. I'll miss Choir. They won't let me be in the concert at the end of term. I won't even have to mime.

Maybe Double Thirteen is special. Maybe one thirteen cancels the other out. Anyway, so far it doesn't seem so bad after all.

Left Foot Forward
Jan Mark

Singlewell High School was small, but St George's C of E Primary had been even smaller. Waiting for his first PE lesson, feeling dwarfish in the high green vaults of the Singlewell changing room, Shaun remembered St George's and felt almost homesick.

In the doorway Mr Durkin loomed. Mr Durkin taught PE and games, and nothing else. At St George's Mrs Calloway had taken them for everything; maths and language, science, cookery, music, art — and football. There were so few of them that to get a team together they used to amalgamate with the boys from Church Whitton and even then Emily Stowe had to be goalie.

Emily was away with the girls now, mutinously playing netball. On the bus home, after the first day at Singlewell, Emily had confided to Shaun that she was going to ask Mr Durkin if she could go on with football, but Shaun, now eyeing Mr Durkin's silhouette, doubted that she would get much encouragement. Mr Durkin reminded Shaun of something out of a horror movie; not the old-fashioned kind where a mad scientist, holed up in a derelict Bavarian **schloss**, created an uncontrollable monster, but the type that turned up on video featuring cybernetic mutants from the future, computerized and ruthless. Seen in that light, Mr Durkin was state of the art.

By the end of the lesson, Shaun realized that he had got it all wrong. Mr Durkin was large but mild. It was Mr Prior, his sidekick, half the size but twice as noisy, who supplied the sound and the fury. Ian Edwards, from Church Whitton, remarked that Durkin and Prior were really an interrogation team, taking turns

---

schloss castle

to soften you up and then rough you up. Ian did not care either way. He was sure of a place in any team going.

Mr Durkin stayed very much in the background while Mr Prior conducted the lesson with a series of barks and grunts. Mr Durkin was watchful; he was on the look-out.

Talent scout, Shaun thought; he's *noticing* people. Ian was noticed, and Tom Carter who had come to Singlewell with Shaun, from St George's. Shaun was noticed too, but in a different way. This became apparent the following Monday, when they had their first games lesson. Sides were chosen. Unlike St George's there were enough of them in the first year for two teams. Shaun was not in either. Mr Prior growled something about acquiring ball skills and sent him, with three other rejects, to kick about on a disused pitch that sloped and had outcrops of rock in it.

'We're the ones with two left feet,' said Edgar Crump, cheerfully, and acquired rock skills, while the other three deployed their six left feet with a mildewed ball that leaked air and, mysteriously, bubbles of moisture. Mr Durkin passed once in their direction, cried, 'That's right; keep it up, lads,' and swerved away again. Shaun, changing afterwards, foresaw that the rest of the term, the rest of the year, possibly the rest of his life was going to be spent like that. Edgar did not mind. He was prepared to wait until May, when his fast bowling would be revealed to the unsuspecting Prior and Durkin. The other two left-footers planned to bring along computer games next time. As far as they were concerned, Monday football constituted an extended lunch hour.

Shaun consulted his timetable and discovered that Monday afternoon was scheduled to end as badly as it had begun. The next lesson was double maths. On his last day at St George's Mrs Calloway had taken him aside and said, 'Don't worry about going to big school. You'll get on fine – but you'll have to work hard at your maths. Promise me you'll do that.'

Shaun had promised. He meant to keep his word and for the first ten minutes of the lesson he paid careful attention, sitting upright with his arms folded upon his new file, with its single sheet of paper on which he had written the date and underlined it neatly. But gradually, like drizzle, a grey memory fell before his eyes; the steep and stony pitch, the flabby ball, the clumsy rejected boots of the eight left feet; new boots, in his case. It did not matter about the others. They didn't care what they played, but he had been looking forward to the games lesson. He loved football. He hated maths. It was going to be a real effort to keep his promise to Mrs Calloway, but he loved football. It had never mattered that the combined team of St George's and Church Whitton had not won a match in three seasons; he enjoyed playing.

The next games period found the eight left feet back on the pitch of stones. Alongside them, on the real pitch, the rest of the group played a real game, while beyond that rose occasional shrieks as Emily Stowe put the fear of God into the netball players.

Edgar had joined the computer freaks, so Shaun had sole possession of the ball, which was no longer round but lopsided, like the **gibbous** moon.

He dribbled it up and down the pitch, pirouetting round flints and tussocks and the strange scaly leaves that sprouted in clumps, alien vegetation from a distant planet. The phantom figures of twenty-one players surrounded him, but he eluded them all, scoring goal after goal. Phantom goalies flung themselves at his headers in futile dives. Phantom team mates hugged him. Occasionally he glanced round to see if Mr Prior or Mr Durkin were looking his way. They never were.

---

gibbous between half and full

On the way back to the changing room a row broke out. Mr Prior had been particularly noisy at close of play. 'Hark at him,' muttered a gingery boy from 1g. 'Anyone would think we were at Wembley. It's only a game.'

A fiery glow seemed to envelop Mr Prior. '*Only a game?* I can't be bothered with people who aren't prepared to give one hundred per cent and then some extra. Only a game? If that's how you feel you can go and play hopscotch. I'm sure we can find someone to take your place.'

Shaun's excitement punched him in the ribs. If they were looking for someone else to take the place of the gingery boy from 1g, there was only one other place where they could look. The same thought occurred to Mr Prior.

'So watch it,' he added lamely.

If only maths did not come next. If only the bad times did not have to happen on Monday afternoons, infecting everything that followed during the rest of the week. English was his best subject; art was fun; geography was easy. He had all three on Monday mornings, a wonderful start to the week. Kind words rang in his ears; complimentary red comments underlined his homework; a sketch of Edgar's feet, which he had knocked off in twenty minutes, ascended miraculously to a place on the wall beside some sixth-former's A level life study. By lunchtime he ought to have been buoyant, confident, set up for success, but the praise was hollow. Beneath the buoyancy lay a dark despondent pit. His self esteem leaked damply away. *After* lunch there was nothing to look forward to but that dismal hour on the pitch of stones, followed by a more dismal hour of maths.

Today was misty. The school, lying on a hillside above the estuary, was swept by coastal squalls, off-shore winds and sea fog. The wet air thickened, white and heavy. The farther goal vanished in the pallid murk; the adjacent pitch was invisible, although

Shaun could tell how the game was going by the surge of noise, ebbing and flowing tidally in the fog; stampeding feet, the thud of boot on ball, the duetting whistles of Prior and Durkin, now close at hand, now fading eerily. Mainly the sounds were at the upper end of the pitch and his heart went out to the lonely goalie on the winning side, marooned in his net at the lower end where he waited for the ball to emerge from the vapour.

After that, the first five minutes of the maths lesson were almost enjoyable. All the lights were on, the radiators were hot. Shaun snuggled down in his corner seat and thawed contentedly, but it could not last. Homework was being handed back. Little was said, but people were looking congratulations at each other as Miss Stevens prowled the classroom, doling out sheets of paper.

'Just proving she knows our names already,' said Ian in front, over his shoulder. 'Show-off.'

'I knew *yours* on the first day,' Miss Stevens said, slapping down his paper in front of him. 'We always notice the loudmouths first. Well done, anyway.'

Ian grinned and turned to pick up his paper. Shaun saw the short hairs on the back of his neck bristle with pride – but now it was Shaun's turn, the last paper of all, limp and forlorn. Shaun looked up at its underside and recognized one of his own dirty thumb prints between Miss Stevens's clean fingertips.

'You don't really seem to have got the hang of this,' Miss Stevens said, laying the paper on his desk so that he could see all the red writing, none of it complimentary this time, that covered it. 'I'll have a word with you at the end of the lesson.'

'Have you always found maths difficult?' Miss Stevens asked, at the end of the lesson.

Shaun nodded, although it was not strictly true. Years ago it had seemed as easy as anything else, in the infants, when it was just something that he did, in those days before it sneakily detached itself from the rest of his education and became maths. But Miss Stevens had BSc. after her name and would not know about the infants.

'Yes, miss,' he said.

Miss Stevens looked kind; sad, but kind. 'I suppose you're one of the bus people.'

He could not see what that had to do with it, whizz-kid Ian was a bus person and it did not seem to do his maths any harm. What he could see, out in the fog, were the headlights of the bus itself, and he had about three minutes in which to catch it.

'Yes, miss.'

'Well then, I can't suggest that you stop after school for extra tuition – some people do that. But you do need help. Are you in the band – or gym club?'

'No, miss.' She certainly did know how to stray off the subject.

'Then you'd better come along to my room tomorrow lunchtime. We'll see how that goes for a few weeks, shall we?'

She was doing him a favour, he knew that. He made a grateful noise and backed out of the room, racing for the cloakroom and then the bus, where Emily Stowe was cock-a-hoop, running up and down the gangway and punching the air. She had been sent off, during netball. No-one in the history of the school, she thought, had ever had a red card in netball.

'It wasn't a foul, though,' she explained, settling next to Shaun as the bus started. 'I'd never do nothing like that. I just throw the ball too hard and no-one can't catch it. They fall over.'

She tried to sound remorseful, but Shaun could envision the other netball players, felled like skittles by Emily's demon delivery.

'I've got to do extra maths,' Shaun said.

'What, for homework?' Emily said. 'I'll help. I'll do it for you.' She had done a lot of it for him at St George's, too. That had been part of the trouble.

'No, at school, Tuesday lunchtime,' Shaun said and saw, with sinking spirits, how the awfulness of Monday was spilling over into Tuesday; how soon, like a creeping paralysis, it would take over Wednesday, and Thursday too, until it ruined the whole week.

When, on the following Monday, Shaun looked at the classroom calendar before registration, he realized that there were only two weeks left before half term. He had heard somewhere that time passes more quickly as you get older. His life was skidding away from under him, and he knew why. At St George's he had taken one day at a time because, except for birthdays and Christmas, or bad moments due to his own villainy, one day had been as good as another. But now he spent his time wishing that Monday was over, even as early as the previous Tuesday. Life had been reduced to a series of Mondays; he scarcely noticed what came in between.

It was a frosty day, clear and bright. From the pitch of stones he could see the estuary glinting in the distance. Weak but well-intentioned sunlight gilded the smoke stacks on the cement works. It was too cold to stand about so the other left feet abandoned the computer games and joined Shaun with the bad-news ball; not the original one which had collapsed altogether and gone strangely stiff, but a replacement, equally limp and soggy. Shaun suspected that somewhere there was a factory turning out special partially-collapsed footballs for people like him.

Indoors again, after they had changed, Mr Durkin read out a list of names. Mr Prior stood by, casting a watchful eye over them.

'All these boys,' he said, 'will report here for extra coaching on Wednesday lunchtimes.' Shaun mentally reviewed the list.

Ian Edwards and Tom Carter were on it, even the gingery boy from 1g. Edgar Crump was not, nor was Shaun, nor any of the other left feet. Those who *were* on it smiled at each other.

'What's them two so pleased with themselves about?' asked Emily Stowe, later, on the bus, as Tom and Ian toasted each other in Seven-Up.

'They've been picked for extra football,' Shaun said.

'I'm going to be let do hockey after half term,' Emily said, 'with the second years.' She paused and thought. 'Why're they doing extra football?'

'Because they're good at it,' Shaun said. 'For the team.'

'But that's not why you get extra maths, is it?' Emily said. 'You get extra maths because you're *not* good at it.'

Shaun felt his gloom pierced by a needle of resentment.

'Yes,' he said.

'Well that's not fair is it?' Emily said. 'You get extra maths because you *can't* do it, and they get extra football because they *can*.'

Shaun's needle became a bodkin, then a six-inch nail.

'If I was you,' Emily advised, with an evil smile, 'I'd ask old Durkin if you can have extra football too.'

He knew that she was not really concerned on his behalf. He had once heard Mrs Calloway describe Emily Stowe as a stirrer. She was stirring now. She liked the idea of a fight.

'You ask him, on Wednesday,' she said. 'I'll come with you.'

Shaun thought that this last was the least attractive proposition he had heard in a long while. But the one before it had certain possibilities.

'I'll ask him by myself,' he said.

'I'll watch,' said Emily.

● ● ● ●

Tuesday's extra maths tuition was not a success. Shaun's mind was on other things. On Wednesday, with Emily at a constant but safe distance, he went along to the changing room, carrying his kit.

Mr Durkin never changed, nor Mr Prior. They seemed to live in their tracksuits, appearing in them for games and PE, at registration and assembly, Mr Prior's small and purple, Mr Durkin's large and black. Shaun approached the large black tracksuit.

'Sir?'

Now, what do you want?' Mr Durkin asked. 'This is extra coaching time.'

'Yes,' Shaun said. 'I know. I want to do extra coaching.'

'No, no,' said Mr Durkin, good-humouredly, as if explaining to an idiot something very obvious, such as how button-holes work. 'This is for the boys who will be in the team.'

'Yes. I want to be in the team,' Shaun said.

He could see Mr Durkin's problem. If Shaun went on like this Mr Durkin would be forced to say, out loud that Shaun had two left feet and might just as well be applying to join the England squad. Out of the corner of his eye he could also see, through the frosted glass panel of the door, Emily Stowe, eavesdropping, longing to rush in and speak up for him. He had to speak up for himself before Emily burst through the door (not bothering to open it but leaving an Emily-shaped hole in the glass, like Desperate Dan) and gazed unblushingly at Ian Edwards and Tom Carter with no trousers on.

'Look, sir,' said Shaun, 'I have to do extra maths with Miss Stevens so I can get good at it. I want to get good at football. I want to do extra, like the others.'

Mr Prior, at this point, might have exploded and seriously damaged Shaun in the blast, but Mr Durkin, fatally, gave himself time to think.

'I'm never going to get good if I don't practise, am I, sir?' Shaun said.

'No-one is stopping you from practising,' Mr Durkin said.

'I can't practise on my own,' Shaun persisted, not on that horrible old pitch with that horrible old ball. Not with people who don't care anyway. I want to play properly. I don't see why I shouldn't do it at all just because I don't do it well. I mean –' he pressed home his advantage '– I mean, I couldn't go to Miss Stevens and say I wasn't going to do that extra maths 'cause I'm no good anyway, could I, sir?'

'That's a bit different,' Mr Durkin said. 'Maths is important. After all, football's only –'

He stopped. He did not say it. Just in time he saw the trap, and it was his own mouth. Then he looked round and saw Mr Prior. Shaun fancied that he detected a light sweat breaking out on Mr Durkin's forehead.

'What's this lad up to?' Mr Prior asked. 'Giving trouble?'

'Not at all,' said Mr Durkin. 'He's just come along to watch the coaching. I think,' said Mr Durkin, and Shaun could see him thinking, 'that shows real enthusiasm, don't you?'

'Yes!' cried Mr Prior, with no enthusiasm at all.

He wheeled, and bolted back to the players. 'Come on, boys. Outside in five seconds flat!'

'Enthusiasm ... important attitude ... essential to team spirit ...' Mr Durkin was chuntering. 'Remind me at the start of the lesson next Monday. I'll see that you get a game – time we tried out some of you others ... oh.' He hesitated. 'I suppose there's no chance that the rest think as you do?'

Shaun smiled kindly.

'What, Edgar and that? Oh no, sir, just me ... I think,' he added, and had the satisfaction of seeing Mr Durkin cringe at the prospect of Edgar and the other left feet taking steps to improve their game.

The Jump
Anthony Masters

I'll run away then, thought Rik as he lay on his bed, his skateboard on the table at his side. His most treasured possession, painted in red and silver but beautifully battered, it was a really fast deck, and he seemed to spend most of his waking hours on it. He thought about skating all the time, and he and his mate Gus were always trying new moves on the wall. They'd mastered the rock 'n roll, the air, the railslide, but there was another one left – one that had defeated them both. The jump was too big, too dangerous, too terrifying for both of them, but Rik planned different ways of tackling it all the time.

Of course it would serve them right, he thought. They'd wonder where he'd gone – maybe get the Old Bill after him. But they wouldn't find him, for at ten Rik knew his way around all right; living in Vauxhall had made it easy for him to know London and its skate parks really well. Nowadays they often went to the South Bank; near the Festival Hall there was a rabbit warren of jumps among the wilderness of concrete. He'd go up there, he decided, skate all day, live rough at night like the homeless people in Cardboard City. That would show his parents a thing or two and make them *really* miss him.

Life had been OK until the baby came along. Helen. It wasn't that he hated her – in fact he had loved her from the start, with her little helpless cries and wriggling limbs – but they loved her more than him. In fact they had stopped loving him completely; Rik was sure of that.

Rik was going through a bit of a crisis anyway, for he had begun to test out his parents, which wasn't going down at all well.

He had been adopted by them when he was four – when they didn't think they could have a baby, he thought grimly. Then a couple of years ago they found they could. It wasn't fair.

Rik had a hazy memory of his earlier life with his real mum, sometimes in the council house in Clapham, or more often in the children's home in Wandsworth. He hadn't spent much time at home, and when he was there Mum was usually drunk or had some guy in. In the end they had taken him away and people came to look at him in the home, a bit like as if they were shopping at Tesco, he supposed.

He could remember feeling very afraid when he had first been adopted and had come to live in the big Victorian flat in Vauxhall, but slowly a history of memories built up with his new mum and dad and he more or less forgot the old life. For a long time it was great; days at Hastings with Mum in the week, football in the park with Dad at weekends, family trips to the cinema, to the swimming pool, to the bowling alley; just the three of them, and it had been good. But now Helen was here and they were four and it wasn't good any longer. The past eighteen months had been lousy with him being shunted more and more into the background.

He had been interested in skateboarding anyway, but directly Rik found he wasn't wanted, it became the central focus of his life – and his school work suffered accordingly.

'Rik!' his mother yelled up the stairs. 'You'll be late. Get on with it!'

Reluctantly he levered himself slowly off the bed and went downstairs, carrying his skateboard. Rik had already made up his mind that he wouldn't go to school that morning. He'd run away instead.

Perhaps it was because Rik wanted to make things worse that everything was so dreadful that morning. First of all he dumped his deck on the floor and Mum stepped on it. In fact she did rather more than that; going completely out of control, with one foot on the deck and the other on the floor, she went into a kind of rattling glide, hit the wainscotting and fell on her back.

'You all right, Mum?' said Rik, laughing and spitting out bits of toast. 'I thought you were trying for a rock 'n roll.'

But she didn't see the funny side of it, and from the look of him neither did Dad.

'That wretched board,' said Mum, struggling to her feet. 'It's going to be the death of me.'

'That's it.' Dad stood up and grabbed the deck. 'That's it then.' He held it in his arms as if it was alive. 'I ought to smash this into a thousand pieces.'

Rik was on his feet now, all laughter forgotten. Dad was in one of his rages and he could be really heavy in one of those.

'Don't, Dad.'

'You've been told not to bring this thing in the house.'

'It's not a thing!'

'Don't be lippy!'

'Give it back!' yelled Rik.

'I beg your pardon, young man?'

'*I said* give it back.'

'Right. It's confiscated.'

'I'll be late for work,' wailed Mum in the background. 'And Helen – she'll be late for her minder. Knock it off, you two.'

Rik was jumping up at his dad like an angry terrier and his dad was holding the skateboard aloft as if it was a trophy.

'Give it, Dad.'

'Get off.'

'It's mine!' Rik managed to grab the edge of his deck and pulled as hard as he could. For a moment it was deadlock, and then Rik wrenched at it again; he caught his dad off balance and he staggered back against a chair. Meanwhile Helen howled as if her lungs would burst.

Rik grasped his prize possession to him and ran through the living room, knocking Mum's purse off the sideboard, and was out into the hallway in seconds.

'Come back,' Dad roared as he thundered behind him. Rik tore at the bolts of the door and for a moment thought the top one was going to stick.

'You'll pay for this.' Dad swiped at him and missed, while Rik pulled open the door and legged it. Then he paused halfway down the garden path and waved his deck at his infuriated father as he stood on the front step.

'I'm not coming back,' Rik bawled.

Dad paused, suddenly realizing that he had gone right over the top. 'Now wait a minute.'

'You'll be sorry!' Rik choked back his angry tears, determined not to give in. 'You'll be sorry when I don't come back. Ever,' he added ominously.

'Let's talk.' Dad was uneasy now, prepared to call a truce, but it was too late.

Rik turned on his heel, but not before he had noticed old nosy Nora Norton twitching at her curtains next door. He gave her a rude sign and ran.

His bravado lasted the walk to the South Bank, but by the time he was almost there, Rik felt deflated and his anger, which had kept him going, had turned to despair. His parents had made him promise never to skate alone, but now he was breaking that promise. They didn't want him. They preferred Helen. No-one cared if he ran away.

But directly he arrived amongst the concrete ramps the jump took over, because it both terrified and fascinated him. He'd never been able to do it and neither had Gus. Nor had any of the bigger boys they had both watched.

Last weekend, Mum and Dad and Helen had come up to watch Rik attempt the jump. He was light and small for his age and thought he had a chance because they were there and he was desperate to show them he could do it. But in the end he had failed, and Dad had put his arm round him, in front of all the skaters, and said, 'It's OK, love – you'll do it when you're bigger.' He had never felt so humiliated in his life and he was sure he could hear muffled laughter. Even Gus had grinned.

But now, as Rik looked at the jump again, all his misery left him. In fact, as usual, he didn't think – couldn't think – of anything else. There was a ramp that ran sheer up a rough concrete support that had never been finished, a short bumpy surface and then at least a four metre drop. It was terrifying, but Rik was convinced that if he got up enough speed he could leap the gap and land on another concrete surface that was narrow and lower. He was sure it was possible, although he had seen many other kids come to grief on it. Either they couldn't make the gradient on the first ramp and simply slid back again, or they actually took off, only to plunge into the abyss. He had done this several times himself and had horribly jarred and scraped himself, but another bigger, heavier boy had broken his leg.

A few yards away the Thames flowed swiftly past, winking and gleaming in the October sunshine. The underneath of the walkways was in shadow, as it always was, and full of graffiti and litter. It smelt of old blankets and bodies and other smells that were more unpleasant and less definable. But Rik noticed none of this. He only had eyes for the jump, and as he sized it up for the hundredth time, Rik felt the familiar stirring of butterflies in his stomach. His mouth went dry, his hands and legs shook and the sweat stood out on his forehead. He was dead scared and knew that what he wanted was that extra bit of courage, the extra confidence that would really make him go for it. Then Rik had a brainwave.

Running away was just what he had needed. What he would do now was practise – all day long if need be – until he made the jump and perfected it. Rik knew that a one-off would not be enough. He had to get it absolutely right so that he could make the jump time after time after time. Then he would ring Gus, tell him where he was and command him to bring his parents up to the South Bank. When they were all there Rik would make his jump to an admiring audience. He could see it now: Mum frightened at first but then building up confidence as he succeeded time after glorious time, her eyes sparkling like the river – just as they had sparkled at him before baby Helen came along and wrecked everything. Dad would be amazingly proud of him and really sorry he had been so horrible. He would shake his hand and not put his arm round him in front of the other skaters. Baby Helen would gurgle with delight and hold out her arms to him and Gus would simply say, 'That was rad.'

The only trouble was that he had to do it first, and the imaginary applause ringing in Rik's ears died away. He stared up at the ramp. As usual it looked impossibly high but this time, because it was a weekday, there was no-one around to provide any competition. Not wanting to waste any time, Rik walked away, got on his deck and built up as much speed as he could, the wheels rasping on the scarred concrete, his breath coming in gasps. By pushing his body from right to left he knew he was building up more speed than usual, and the panic rose from the pit of his stomach as he soared up the ramp, launched off, bent down, grabbed the bottom of the deck, let go – and just failed to make contact with the other side. He fell sideways, bashing his shoulder on the raw concrete, feeling his skin burn, and then landing upside down in a sea of stinking litter.

Rik lay there for a few seconds, wondering what he had broken. Then he moved gingerly and discovered that although his shoulder was smarting he seemed to be intact. He had always been good at gym at school and knew instinctively how to fall, and of course he was so light. Thankfully Rik picked himself up and started all over again.

He stayed working at it for the next hour, but every time he skated up the ramp his courage failed him and he managed to stop himself at the brink, poised on his deck on the narrow ledge, staring down at the abyss below him in horror. Then, using every last ounce of courage he had left, Rik got up speed again and on reaching the top, bent down without grabbing the deck and took off into the air. This time he crashed down on his feet, his deck following him, clunking him painfully on the head as it crashed to the ground. Trembling, jarred, sweating and virtually in tears, Rik stood in the filthy gully, looking up at the high, bleak sides of concrete above him, feeling angry and defeated.

Later, Rik walked over to Casey Jones at Waterloo station and using his school dinner money bought himself a bag of chips and a small orangeade. That completely cleaned him out and he felt very depressed as he walked back to the South Bank. His father's words echoed in his head, he had not yet got anywhere near mastering the jump and he could imagine his parents coming home from work, petting Helen and forgetting all about him.

'He'll come home when it suits him,' he could hear his mother saying, while his father added censoriously, 'That boy needs a good hiding – and he'll get it!'

Throughout the afternoon Rik continued to practise, but his nerve had now gone completely and he could only skate up the ramp – and roll miserably back. By four he was feeling exhausted, and by five sick and terribly hungry. His stomach rumbled and his head felt muzzy, yet Rik kept trying, going up the ramp time after time – and still rolling back. By half past five he thought he was going to faint and his whole body ran with a sticky sweat, but by six he had a second wind and he felt stronger both physically and mentally.

It was getting cold now and shadows moved underneath the walkways as the homeless clambered into sleeping bags if they were lucky and under newspapers and cardboard if they weren't. I'll be sleeping with this lot tonight, thought Rik – at least, I will be if I don't make the jump. I'll never make it, he thought gloomily and with mounting desperation, never ever make it. He looked round again at the dim figures settling into Cardboard City and wondered if they'd be friendly to be with or whether they would chuck him out just like his dad had done. Why don't they come and find me, thought Rik suddenly and the tears pricked at the back of his eyes. He might as well have been back in the children's home, feeling unwanted and uncared for.

Parents – they were all the same: hostile and unreliable – they'd desert you in the end. A tear trickled down Rik's grubby cheek and then another, but he brushed them away angrily, a renewed determination coming over him. He'd crack that jump by the time the light faded or die in the attempt.

A few other skaters had turned up and he tried to look cool and not exhausted in front of them. They gave him the impetus to summon up more courage or be shown up, and he went up the ramp even faster than he had done before, a new recklessness coming over him. This time he yanked the deck on to the ramp with his legs and at least half of it hit the concrete across the chasm. But it wasn't enough, and he fell backwards into the stinking pit and hit his head on an abandoned wooden box. It was this that saved him from serious injury; otherwise his head would have been cracked open on the unyielding concrete.

Rik struggled to his feet, dazed and shocked, but no-one came up to him or even sympathized with his fall. The skaters just continued their railslides and 180s and 360s and grabs and moves, although no-one, he noticed, attempted the jump. Rik stood there, gazing at them bleakly and then returned to his old cycle of dashing up the ramp and pulling back at the last moment. This seemed to last an eternity until Rik's second wind started running out and he knew it was hopeless, that he'd never succeed in mastering the jump before dark. Still determined not to go home and admit defeat, he felt sick and afraid, knowing he would have to face hours in Cardboard City before first light.

Gradually, as the shadows lengthened, the other skaters went away and Rik was alone again, still trying, but still holding back at the edge while the sweat ran into his eyes, continually blinding him. He realized that by now he must stink as much as the pit he was trying to cross, but he didn't care. Again he got his deck at high speed, again he went up the ramp, again he faltered at the brink.

Then he saw them, standing in a half circle in the gloom. His own desperate concentration and the hooting of boats on the river must have concealed the sound of their arrival. They had closely-shaved heads, gaudy clothes, chains, tight torn jeans and were wearing roller-boots. All were about sixteen; all were grinning and mocking him.

'We been watching you,' said one of the gang who had a spike through his nose. 'What you doing then?'

'It doesn't matter.'

'Come on!'

'Just skating.'

'Why do you keep going up that ramp? You're not getting anywhere,' said another with a bright orange scarf in his hair.

'I'm all right.'

'You a nutter?' asked a third. They began to move in and the one with the spike through his nose took off his roller-boots and walked over to Rik.

'Let's have a go.'

Rik picked up his deck and backed up against a pillar.

'Come on.'

'I don't let anyone on my deck.'

'But you'll let me.' He was very close now and Rik knew he was in dead trouble.

'No,' he said defiantly.

'That's not nice.'

The rest of the gang were grinning away now.

'I said – no.'

'Let's have it.'

'Get lost!'

'He's not nice, is he?' said the boy, turning round to his audience who moved in still further. 'Not nice at all. Now give it here.'

'No way.' Rik was almost crushed into the concrete now, his deck hugged to his chest. 'Hang on!'

Someone stepped out of the shadows – and then someone else. They were big men, in their thirties, dressed in sweat shirts and jeans with tattoos running down the rippling muscles of their arms. One had a beard, the other, slightly younger, was clean shaven, and it was he who was doing the talking.

'What's going on?'

'Nothing,' said the roller-booter with the spike through his nose.

'You having a go at this kid?'

'No.'

'I think you are.'

'Only asked him if I could have a go on his deck.'

'Can't you take a hint? He doesn't want you to, does he? Look – he's practically disappearing into the concrete.'

'I only asked –'

'Yeah. Now clear off!'

Both the big men advanced on the roller-booters who began to back off. Hastily, the boy with the spike through his nose put his roller-boots back on.

'All right. All right.'

'Move!'

'We're going.'

They turned tail and rollered away, making sure they cheered and catcalled from a safe distance. Then they were gone.

'You look all in, kid,' said the younger of the tattooed men. 'And relax, we're not gonna take your board. We were watching you trying your jump. It'll come off one day. But you should go home now. It gets dodgy round here late at night.'

'Can't go home,' said Rik, emerging from his pillar.

'Why not?' asked the older man. He spoke with a gravelly voice and didn't seem to be so friendly. 'You shouldn't be around here on your own.'

'Gotta get this right first.'

'Wait a minute.' The younger man eyed him curiously. 'Why is it so important?'

'Just is.'

'And you can't go home till it's done?'

'No.'

'I was like you as a kid. Persistent. My name's Harry. This is my mate Dennis. We're not going to stay long – and you shouldn't really be talking to us, not to strangers like – so I'm gonna give you a piece of advice and then clear off. Right?'

Rik stared at them, still clutching his skateboard, as wary of them now as he had been of the rollerbooters. Suddenly he nodded and said, 'What's your advice then?'

'My kid brother tries jumps like this, real hard ones, and he always takes his deck a long way back. His trick is – more speed and a hard shove before he goes over. That's how he does it. So why don't you give it a try?'

Rik hesitated. Harry made it all sound so easy. His kid brother came across as a right little know-all, and yet...

'Go on, the longer run gives you more speed, and as you come off the ramp let the deck do the work. That should do it.' Harry's voice was warm and enthusiastic, willing Rik to do it, and his enthusiasm was catching. 'Why don't you give it a whirl?'

'Yes,' said Rik reluctantly.

'One other thing you need to do, kid.' Dennis suddenly came to life and for once he didn't sound mocking. 'Believe in yourself.' He laughed harshly but his eyes were as warm and encouraging as Harry's. 'Go for it, kid. Remember what he said – and go. Now. Before you change your mind.'

Rik took his skateboard as far back as he could. Then he went for it, feeling the others' confidence almost as if it was inside him, like a warm glow that was willing him on. He had never travelled so fast on his deck before and he hit the ramp with tremendous speed. But despite this his head remained cool and calm and he did exactly what Harry had told him to do and, when he came to the edge of the abyss, letting the deck do all the work, it zoomed across the gap, striking the concrete fair and square, well away from the edge. He'd done it. He was amazed – but he'd done it.

A burst of applause came not only from Harry and Dennis but from dozens of people he couldn't see, crouched in their newspapers and cardboard and bedding.

'I did it, Harry,' yelled Rik.

'Sure you did.' Harry was very laid back. 'Now come round here and do it again. Prove it wasn't a one-off.'

Grinning, Rik came back and did as he was told.

In all Rik successfully made the jump five times, and he gathered more confidence each time, despite the fact that it was nearly dark. It was on the sixth that he noticed a little group of spectators had built up on the river walk – and standing at the back of them was a familiar figure. It was his dad. When he saw that Rik had seen him he came slowly forward.

'Dad!'

He looked very haggard as he grabbed Rik by the shoulder. Harry and Dennis grinned and walked slowly away.

'Where've you been? I've looked all over. I've been to every skateboard park –'

'Did you see what I did? It was the jump I couldn't do. I did it, Dad!'

His father took no notice. 'Do you realize how worried me and your mother have been? Anything could have happened to you.'

'I've been practising all day,' said Rik who was hardly listening. 'Then these blokes showed me.' He turned round but saw they'd gone. 'Watch me now.'

But his father put out a restraining hand as Rik prepared to go into action for the seventh time. 'You're coming home.'

'Am I in trouble?'

He paused and then said slowly, 'It's our fault just as much as yours.'

'Wish Mum could see me do the jump.'

His father suddenly grinned. 'She will and all.'

'When?' Rik was suspicious.

'Tomorrow morning. We'll all take the day off.'

'*What?*'

'I'll drive the whole lot of you up here so you can show that jump to me and Mum and Helen. Would you like that?'

'Yeah!'

'Come on then.'

Rik stared into the darkness of Cardboard City. A little wind rattled the litter and sent a Coke can rolling and clattering on the pavement. Rik looked at the jump confidently; he knew he could do it again.

No Sweat
Michelle Magorian

Mark walked out of the men's changing room to the big pool. At the end of the roped-off lanes, under the Charity Swimathon banner, sat men and women with clipboards. Like the attendants they were wearing red Swimathon T-shirts.

Mark stood uncertainly for a moment. He had been told his lane was the second one in from the far side. He walked alongside the pool past the white plastic chairs to where a young man was sitting.

'Are you the lap counter for the 12–14 group?' he asked.

'Yes. Which one are you?'

'Mark. Mark Stevens.'

The man ticked his name. 'Where's the rest of your team?'

'They're coming later. I'm swimming the first 200 lengths and they're sharing the next hundred between them.'

The man nodded.

No sweat, thought Mark.

Mark sat down, his towel draped round his shoulders. Not that he needed it. It was boiling. He twisted the red bathing-cap they had distributed to all the participants and gazed past the rows of flags, which had been hung above the pool, towards the clock. Nearly two. He dropped his shoulders and blew out a few breaths. Relax, he told himself.

Just then pop music began blaring out of two speakers. He shaded his eyes with his hands. Even though it was daytime the lights seemed brighter than usual, and there were more of them. He glanced across at the balloons decked out over the boarded-out baby pool. Already people were sitting there at white tables and chairs drinking tea or fruit juice.

To his surprise his stomach was already fluttering. He mustn't get too nervous. Nerves could exhaust you.

He began to take in the teams on either side of his lane. Looking at them through Jacko and Terry's eyes he couldn't help grinning.

On one side was a team of four youths between 16 and 18 years old. A short stocky man in his 40s wearing a peaked cap was giving them a pep talk, revving them up and waving a stopwatch. Mark guessed they were from a youth club. Boy scout stuff.

He, Jacko and Terry didn't need to join a club. They just got on and did things. No sweat.

Knowing that he was at least four years younger than the team of youths, Mark felt very superior. Just look at them, he thought, hanging on to the coach's every word, looking as serious as if they were entering the Olympics.

The young men began shaking their legs, warming up. Daft that they were all there at the same time, Mark thought. The ones that were third and fourth would be worn out from watching before they had begun.

He glanced at the team on the other side. He couldn't see anyone at first. And then he did.

She was an elderly woman with cropped grey hair. A wrinkly!

He smothered a laugh. He was going to be swimming next to a bunch of wrinklies! He could hear Jacko and Terry's shrieks and feel their powerful elbows crashing into his ribs with mirth.

He looked down hastily. He mustn't get an attack of laughter. He'd never get through one length if he did.

Out of the corner of his eye he watched her take off a heavy purple towelling robe and pull on her Swimathon bathing-cap. Embarrassing to go around in a swim-suit at her age.

'Attention everyone!' a voice rang out.

Mark sat up straight.

This was it.

A tall man in his 50s was addressing them. Mark knew the rules. He didn't have to hear them. He, Jacko and Terry had studied them enough in the sports-centre canteen. No sweat.

Before long he saw the man approach him.

'On your own?' he asked.

'The rest of my team are coming later.'

'He's doing a hundred,' said Mark's lap counter.

'How old are you?'

'Twelve,' nearly, he added inside his head. 'The others are fourteen.'

The man smiled. 'Good on you.'

To Mark's annoyance he felt a flush of pleasure. He shrugged off the man's remark.

'You'll notice some of the teams will be swimming very fast,' said the man. 'Don't let that bother you. Go at your own pace.'

Mark nodded.

'Hello Joan,' said the man, and he waved at the old woman next to him. 'Back again?'

So the wrinkly's name was Joan. Mark shut his ears to their conversation and looked up at the clock.

He could swim a length a minute up to about thirty lengths and then he'd begin to slow down.

Two hours, he reckoned. Two hours of swimming. Not the best way of thinking about it. He must pace himself, length by length and keep adding up how much money he could raise for the children's hospital.

Nice to think he'd be earning money by doing something he enjoyed.

'Everyone ready?' said the man in charge.

The coach on his left had his hand on the shoulder of the first youth.

'You can do it,' he was saying firmly.

'Wally,' muttered Mark. He was going to be swimming half the distance Mark was going to swim. Mark pulled on his hat and slipped off his towel.

He heard the wrinkly lower herself into the water. The rest of her team would probably be hobbling in hours later. That is if they hadn't pegged out first.

He was grinning again. Concentrate, he told himself firmly.

He stood up and slipped into the water.

To his surprise he felt tired. After only one length he was ready to get out. Perhaps breast-stroke was the wrong one to choose. But it was his best stroke. He'd never be able to do the crawl for a hundred lengths.

A high wave from the youth in the next lane sent a gallon of chlorine down Mark's throat and into his eyes. He coughed, gasping for breath. This was a disaster.

Relax, he told himself.

By the third length he'd got his wind back, but he still felt wiped out. He'd steered to the side of the lane, away from the Olympic youth who was crawling at high speed and making waves all around him. The wrinkly was a more sedate swimmer.

It wasn't till he was ten lengths in that the tiredness dissipated. With relief he realized that he had been warming up in the water. That and shaking off his nerves. He had also worked out a steady rhythm. One that he felt would carry him to a hundred.

Now he was enjoying himself. He had started to glide. There was nothing to think about, nothing to worry about. There was just him and the water, the bright lights, the pumping music, the loud splashing and the reverberating voices of the spectators. The noise was deafening.

The first forty lengths were a doddle. It was around his forty-second length when the coach in the next lane started yelling at the youth in the water. 'You can do it! You can do it!'

The three other youths were yelling too, fit to bust. It annoyed Mark, the big deal they were making of it.

Mark couldn't see the youth's head, just a flurry of water drawing closer to the end of the lane. The coach pressed his stop-watch and the next youth lowered himself in. Within seconds the coach had a towel round the first youth's shoulders and was sending someone off to get hot chocolate like he'd climbed Mount Everest.

Mark turned and pushed off, glancing round for Jacko and Terry. No sign of them yet. Still, there was plenty of time.

It was when the second youth was being urged on to swim faster that the penny dropped. They weren't getting worked up about the number of lengths they were swimming. It was the time they were taking to swim them. They were obviously trying to win some record for speed. That's what all the excitement was about.

As Mark touched the side of the bath, his lap counter looked up. 'Twelve lengths to go,' he said.

And there was no Jacko and no Terry. They had to arrive soon otherwise Mark's hundred lengths wouldn't even be counted, and his team would be disqualified.

Three months of working himself up to a hundred lengths down the tube. And would his sponsors pay up if their team hadn't done the two hundred lengths?

As he turned at the end of the pool, someone put a new tape on. The sound blasted out of the two speakers so loudly it nearly knocked him over.

As Mark headed back towards his lap counter, he realized that part of what had driven him to do a hundred lengths was the desire to impress Jacko and Terry. It was important that they knew he was as tough as them, even though they were approaching six feet and broad-shouldered with it. They had to be there to see him swim that hundred lengths. Be there to show their amazement and slap him on the back even though it stung like a burn when they did it. Then he'd be one of them. They would be a trio, not a duo and a hanger-on. He would never feel lost for words with them again and he'd be able to make jokes as brilliantly as them.

Ninety-eight lengths, two to go.

To his annoyance he felt a stab of jealousy for the team in the next lane. Not for their swimming ability, he was as good, but because they had mates rooting for every length they swam.

No one was even noticing Mark, aside from the lap counter, who he realized now wasn't allowed to flicker a face muscle.

It was then that he remembered the wrinkly. She was still swimming too. He had been so wrapped up in himself that he hadn't noticed that her team hadn't shown up either.

Mark swam slowly towards the end of the lane. His heart sinking, his fingers touched the wall.

'A hundred,' said the lap counter.

Mark rested his arms over the end.

'What are you going to do?' asked the man.

Mark had a lump in his throat the size of a fist. Do, he thought, do? Cry my bloody eyes out, that's what he felt like doing.

'Sorry, I'm afraid your hundred doesn't count,' he continued.

Mark nodded miserably.

Next to him the youths were whistling and cheering. If only they'd shut up and the music was turned down, he could think more clearly.

A refined voice pierced through his misery.

It was the wrinkly.

'What's up?' she asked.

None of your business, you old prune, he whispered angrily inside his head.

'His team hasn't turned up.'

'Can't he keep swimming till they do?'

'He's already swum a hundred.'

'I know.' She turned to him. 'I've been watching you out of the corner of my eye. You've done marvellously. Come on, keep going. You can give me moral support.'

'Where's your team?' he asked.

She pointed to herself. 'I'm my team. I'm trying for the two-hundred-lengths certificate.'

'Two hundred? But that's three miles,' and he stared at her, stunned.

'And a bit.'

'Sorry,' he added quickly, realizing his jaw was still open.

But he couldn't help himself. A wrinkly going for two hundred lengths!

She laughed.

Mark looked up at his lap counter. 'Can I?'

'Sure, if you think you can manage it.'

'They'll be here soon, I know they will. They've never let me down before. I expect they've been held up somewhere.'

The man nodded.

'Let's go,' said the woman, smiling.

And Mark, in spite of his desire to remain Mr Cool, found himself smiling back.

They pushed themselves on.

Now he really *would* need to pace himself.

He consciously relaxed his shoulders again and pushed more firmly with his legs. No, he thought, his mates had never let him down. Come to think of it, though, he'd never asked them to do anything before. But he hadn't asked them. They'd volunteered. No sweat, they had said. Fifty lengths. Dead easy.

So what had happened to them? He pictured them lying in a pool of blood on Wembley High Street, gasping out some garbled message to the ambulancemen about telling Mark they couldn't make it, but both sinking into unconsciousness before their vital message could be understood.

He touched the wall and turned.

A hundred and one.

Take it easy, he told himself. They'll be here. There's probably been a hold-up on the tube. They were always having trouble on their line. They were probably stuck somewhere, unable to ring the sports centre because the nearest phones had been vandalized. They'd be in a right stew, cursing and pacing the platform and punching walls.

A hundred and two lengths.

He blew heavily into the water. They could be ill of course. Both of them? No. Unless it was food poisoning from a take-away kebab or pizza. Yes, they were probably heaving up somewhere, unable even to keep down a teaspoon of water, struggling to get to the door, picking up their towels, all strength gone, but still determined to make it.

A hundred and three lengths.

When Mark swam his hundred and fiftieth length he knew that Jacko and Terry weren't going to make it. He turned over on to his back. His neck ached so painfully that he thought it would crack. He'd done a hundred and fifty useless lengths. Useless because in no way could he swim any further. If he could get out and have a break he might make it to two hundred, but it wouldn't count.

He was past caring now. He was so tired he could hardly breathe. He'd take a rest doing a slow backstroke before climbing out.

Joan was still going. He had to call her Joan now. Wrinkly was the word Jacko and Terry used for anyone elderly and it didn't suit her. He glanced aside at her. She had more guts, stamina and strength than the two of them rolled together. He pictured them making their comments in their trendy jeans and latest trainers and jackets. Legs just that little too far apart, macho men. Hey, Marko, we forgot. He could hear them saying it. No hard feelings, eh? Slam of hand on shoulder. You know how it is? Yeah, thought Mark. I know how it is. Next year, eh? Yeah, next year, or the year after.

He smiled bitterly. His so-called mates had never intended coming at all. Oh yeah, we can do this. Oh yeah, we can do that. No sweat.

And that summed them up. No sweat. They were incapable of producing a drop of it because they didn't do anything. They were all talk.

Yet he had longed to be one of them. Longed to stop feeling tongue-tied and small and boring. But it wasn't him that was boring. He had just been bored in their company. Bored, bored, bored.

A hundred and fifty-one.

Why hadn't he seen through them before? How come he had believed all their blether? As he lay on his back, a new emotion swept through him. Anger. Anger at them. And anger with himself. As soon as he touched the wall he turned over and began to crawl. He still knew he wouldn't make it, but at least moving his neck from side to side would ease the pain. He lashed out furiously into the water like a tiger released from captivity. Wild and powerful, yet still in control. Still graceful.

As he crawled length after length he swam out all the feelings he had kept bottled up inside him for months. All the doubts he had ignored when Jacko and Terry never turned up for a practise with him, but told him they were practising on other days. How could he have been so stupid? Because he was desperate to have friends. Any friends.

Almost the dullest in his class, but not quite. Never feeling he could mix with the dumbos or the ones that got by. Switched off and switched out. That was him.

A hundred and seventy lengths.

The team beside him had finished. They were jubilant.

Well-pleased with themselves.

Joan was still swimming. As *if* she sensed him looking at her she beamed at him. 'Think I'll make it?' she yelled.

'Yeah, 'course you will.' He nearly said, no sweat, but stopped himself.

His neck had eased up now. His shoulders and ankles ached instead. He rolled over into the back-stroke again to give himself another rest.

● ● ● ●

By the time Mark completed his one hundred and eightieth length there was no one left in the pool except him and Joan. The only people around the pool were their two lap counters and a life-guard on a high-seated podium at the side.

The man who was in charge came out of the office and gazed in Mark's direction.

Don't say he's going to disqualify me now, thought Mark. But the man grinned and raised two thumbs. He was rooting for him! He gave Joan the same message.

It was then that Mark noticed that the life-guard was smiling. Mark hadn't even bothered to look at him. And he gave a thumbs-up sign too! Three people wanted him to make it. It pushed him to complete the next length.

Soon after this incident, attendants came out of the office, curious to watch Joan and him. They appeared relaxed and not at all bothered at having to stay behind.

The early evening sun had found its way to a long window at the side and it streamed into the pool. Someone had turned the music off. It was so quiet that Mark could hear the water lapping around him. He could have been swimming in a private pool in Malibu.

Two attendants were removing the flags above their heads.

'Take your time,' said his lap counter, picking up Mark's anxiety. 'Keep to your own steady pace, we're not in a hurry.'

Ten lengths to go and he knew. He knew he was going to make it.

Please don't let me pass out, get cramp or die, he told himself.

Attendants had begun to gather round his lap counter who was now fighting down a smile.

'Come on, you're nearly there,' shouted a tall blond-haired girl.

Mark nearly choked. Jacko and Terry had been lusting after her for weeks. They never said hello to her of course. They just stared at her and talked about her. And here she was rooting for him, twelve years old, nearly, and puny. Correction, he told himself. Puny people don't swim a hundred and ninety-two lengths. Three miles!

He laughed. He had no friends and he was laughing. Crazy. But he decided he'd rather be himself and have no friends than try and pretend to be someone he wasn't. And it made him feel feather-light.

It was the last length and it was so sweet he didn't want to rush it. Joan knew and she cheered from the water. And then everyone round the pool was clapping. And the man in charge was clasping his hands above his head.

Mark came in on a leisured crawl, touched the side and hung there, high. He swam to the steps at the side. He was too weak to pull himself out of the pool from the water. He had hardly reached the chairs when his legs buckled. He sat down quickly and wrapped the towel around his aching shoulders. His legs were shaking.

His ankles ached and his feet felt as though someone had stuck them in a fridge. All he wanted to do was collapse into bed and sleep.

'Two hundred lengths,' said his lap counter, smiling.

Mark nodded, still trying to catch his breath. The man in charge grinned down at him.

'Looks like you didn't need your team-mates after all.'

'Yeah,' he agreed.

The man handed him an orange juice. Mark held it for a moment and then sipped it slowly. He wanted to sit still and take in what he had achieved. 'Two hundred lengths,' he whispered. 'I have just swum two hundred lengths.' He had proved something to himself. He wasn't sure what, but it felt very good.

'You'd best get dressed before you get too cold,' said the lap counter.

'Not yet,' said Mark, putting down the beaker.

'It's over now.'

'Not for Joan it isn't.' And he pulled himself shakily to his feet, stumbled over to her lane and started yelling.

Going Up
Robert Swindells

It was going to be the most exciting day of my life when Barfax Town played Lincoln City away in the last game of the season. If we won, Barfax would be promoted to the First Division for the first time since my dad was a kid. The whole town buzzed with it for a fortnight. You could feel the tension, just walking through the streets.

We had our tickets and seats on the coach. Dad and me, I mean. We never went to away matches but we were off to this one, no danger. Part-time supporters Dale always calls us, but it's not that. Dad works Saturday mornings so it's impossible for him to get away in time. He'd got special permission this time though, like a lot of other guys in Barfax.

Dale's my brother. He's a red-hot Town supporter. Goes to every match, but not with Dad and me. He's sixteen and part of the Ointment. The Ointment are the Barfax headbangers, feared by every club in the land according to him. Dad reckons they're a bunch of tossers and Dale should kick 'em into touch but he won't. Dead loyal to Lud, see? Lud Hudson, leader of the Ointment and cock of the Barfax Kop.

Was, I should say. *Was* loyal, till all that stuff went down at Lincoln. A right mess, that was. Total bummer. If you're not doing anything special I'll tell you all about it.

First thing was, Dad lost his half day off. Big job came in at work and that was that. 'Sorry, Tel,' he goes. 'Can't be helped.'

My name's Terry but everybody calls me Tel. And yes I *know* I should've said, 'Ah well, it's only a game,' but I didn't. I went ballistic instead. Well, this was Thursday, right? *Two flipping days* before the match, and I'd been building up to it for a fortnight. 'S'not fair,' I screeched. 'Everyone else is off, why not me? Our Dale's going.'

And that's when I got this brilliant idea. I could go with Dale, couldn't I? I eyeballed Dad through my tears. 'Why can't *Dale* take me – he's my brother, isn't he?' You could see he wasn't keen. Dad, I mean. He sighed, pulled a face.

'Our Dale ... he's not *reliable,* Tel. It's those headbangers he knocks around with. I wouldn't feel easy in my mind...'

Easy in your mind? Wow, did I let rip. What about *my* mind? What about I've been looking forward to this match for *two weeks?* Why should *I* stay home while all my mates're there, shouting for the Town? They'll show off, Monday. Laugh at me. I won't dare show my face at school.

And he gave in. Against his better judgement, he said, but I didn't care. I was over the moon.

Our Dale wasn't. He went ape-shape. '*Tel?*' he yelps when Dad mentions it. 'Drag our *Tel* along? You're joking. My mates. Lud ... I'll be a laughing stock, Dad. They'll *crucify* me.'

Poor old Dad. Not only was he missing the match himself, he was getting all this grief from the two of us as well. Don't think I'll have any kids when I grow up. Anyway, he lays into our Dale, tells him at sixteen it's time he started taking a bit of responsibility and all that, and in the end the big plonker agrees to take me. No choice really.

So. The big day rolled round at last, and at half eleven there I was in my Town scarf and cap, trotting at my brother's heels towards the coach park. He was going fast on purpose but I wasn't bothered. I'd have stuck with him somehow if he'd been Lynford flipping *Christie.* The road was crammed with folk in scarves and caps, all heading the same way. I bet most of 'em had never been to a match before in their lives.

You should've seen the coach park. Talk about seething. There must've been at least twelve coaches, and that's not counting all the people who were going by train or car. Dale heads straight for the Ointment coach. They don't have their own, I don't mean that, but they must've planned in advance to take one over because there they were in a mob by the door, shouting and laughing, stopping other folk from getting near. I don't suppose many people fancied travelling with them anyway.

'Hey up, Dale – started a day nursery, have you?' A great husky guy in black, studded leather looks from Dale to me and back to Dale.

My brother grins, sheepishly. 'Naw, just minding our Tel for the day. You know how it is.'

'You mean ... Tel here's travelling with *us*?'

'Well, yeah, just this once. My old man...'

'Sod your old man. What if...?'

'Hey, mind your language, Lud. I'll just have to...you know... stay out of it if it happens, that's all.'

'Stay *out* of it?' He scowled at my brother. Others were chuckling, nudging one another. I wished Dad was with us. 'Now you listen here, my son. You stay out today, you're *out*, geddit? Ointment don't *choose* when to rumble. Ointment's there for its mates, for the *Town*, see? Town pride, is what it's all about. You think about that all the way down, son, 'cause there ain't no *nannies* in the Ointment.'

He was great, that Lud. I mean, I *know* he was a thug, but you should've seen how he controlled those headbangers. They *worshipped* him. Nobody else could've done it.

It was terrific, that coach ride. See – to really enjoy a match there's got to be atmosphere, and those guys really knew how to build atmosphere. It was the jokes and the songs, especially the songs. What they did was, they started yelling for the kids in various parts of the bus to give them a song. You know – *back seat back seat sing us a song, back seat – sing us a song.* The kids on the back seat would sing a song, then it'd be, *front end front end sing us a song* – and so on. Just after Doncaster we ran over a dog, and like a flash they crowded up to the back window going, *dead dog dead dog sing us a song* – horrible I know, but magic too. I've never felt so fired up in my life.

We got to Lincoln just after one. The police were waiting to escort the Town fans, but Lud knew an alleyway and the Ointment slipped into it. Dale had ignored me on the coach and he ignored me now. I had to run to keep up as they negotiated the alley and headed for a pub they knew opposite the ground.

I'd never been in a pub. I didn't know kids could. I plucked at Dale's sleeve. 'I can't go in there. I don't want to.'

'Shut it, kid. You're with me, you go where I go. Come on.'

The place was packed. Smoky. They barged in, shouting and swearing, intimidating customers into making room for them. Nobody took any notice of me, it was like I wasn't there. All these bodies jostling, shoving me around. I couldn't see over them. It was taking me all my time to keep from falling. I was sweating like a pig and the smell of the place made me feel sick.

After a bit they found some seats – I think people left to get away from us – and Dale put me on a bench between two of the guys. He'd got me a Coke and some crisps. I thought, this is better. It's going to be all right now. They were talking about the match. Next season in the first division. Cheering and laughing, slurping pints. Dale had given over telling them to mind their language. I sat there and tried to be part of the Ointment.

It might have been OK if a crowd of Lincoln fans hadn't showed up. Twenty-past two and in they came in their colours, roaring. They knew we were there, and the Ointment had been expecting them. They leapt up, overturning chairs, knocking glasses and beermats on the floor, surging towards their challengers. In a second I went from being crammed in to having the whole bench to myself. I didn't know what I was supposed to do. *You're with me you go where I go.* Was I meant to join the fight?

It *was* a fight, over there by the door. A terrible fight. Crashing and yelling and the sound of things breaking. The customers had fled out the back. There was just the fight, and a guy behind the bar on the phone, and me. I couldn't move. I sat there wishing I'd stayed home. I didn't care about the match any more, I just wanted to be somewhere familiar. Somewhere safe.

There was a noise, over the noise of fighting. Sirens. The Ointment and the Lincoln lads crammed the doorway, struggling to get out of the pub while continuing to knock hell out of one another. I looked for Dale but couldn't see him. He'd forgotten me. I was alone in a city I didn't know. A city full of enemies.

Suddenly the pub was empty. A guy charged over a sea of broken glass, aimed a kick at a youth in the doorway and the pair of them swayed snarling out of sight. I slipped off the bench and ran to the door, yelling for my brother. Two police cars stood at the kerb, blue lights flashing. The fight was a few metres away down the street. A woman somewhere screamed.

Dogs came out of a white van. Police dogs on leads, pulling their handlers towards the battle. The fighters broke and ran, all except one who stood bent over, blood pouring from between the fingers he'd clamped to his face. It wasn't Dale. I started in the direction the fight had gone because I didn't know what else to do. I had my ticket, but I couldn't remember where the coaches were picking us up after. How could I watch a soccer match, knowing I was lost a hundred miles from home?

It was then I heard my name. 'Terry? What're you doing here? Where's your dad?' I turned, weak with relief. It was Popo, Dad's mate, with Danny his son, same age as me.

I shook my head. 'Dad couldn't come. Work. I'm with Dale, but he's…' I gestured towards the dog handlers. 'He's somewhere, fighting.'

'Oh, I see. Oh dear. Well, you'd better come with us, I think. Never know when Dale might … got a ticket, have you?'

'Yes.' I got it out, showed him. I'd never been so pleased to see anyone in my life.

He nodded, smiled. 'Come on then. We'll see Dale inside, I expect.'

We didn't though. Popo sat me and Danny on a rail so we could see over people's heads, and all through the match I kept looking round for my brother, except the last ten minutes when it got too nail-biting and I forgot. They were torture, those last ten minutes. We seemed to be heading for a goalless draw – missing out on promotion by two rotten points – when a Lincoln player fouled Billy Watson and the ref awarded Town a free kick just outside the box. Watson took it himself and it was a beauty, swerving round the end of their wall and ricocheting off the underside of the bar into the top right hand corner of the net. Half a centimetre higher and it'd have bounced out. You should've heard us roar. You probably *did* – it's only a hundred miles after all. Anyway there were ten minutes left and they chucked everything at us. I'm not kidding – even their *goalie* had a shot. Well, they'd nothing to lose and everything to gain, but it was no use. Our lads hung on and that's how we went up.

Popo drove me home. Danny and I clamped our scarves in the windows so they flapped in the slipstream all the way up the A1.

That's the good news. The bad news is that Dale didn't make it home that night, and poor Lud didn't make it at all. Somebody stabbed him and he died in hospital without ever knowing the result of the match. None of the Ointment saw the game. By the time Watson swerved us into Division One they were all down the police station being charged. It was Sunday lunchtime when our Dale turned up. He'd come by train, and he was breathing funny owing to bruised ribs. Dad had intended giving him hell for leaving me, but he looked so rough he let him stagger off to bed.

Monday teatime we're all in the front room watching telly. Town on an open top bus getting a civic reception, but when the chairman comes on our Dale gets up and leaves the room because he knows what he's going to say. Naturally he starts by regretting Lud's tragic death, but then he says, 'Those youths who brawled on the streets of Lincoln last Saturday are not our supporters. They have no share in our triumph and are not welcome on our terraces. We are a First Division club with First Division fans. There is no place in our ranks for scum.'

A bit later on I go up to the toilet and pass Dale on the landing and he's been crying. 'Have I heck,' he says when I mention it, but he has. He's had the telly on in his room and heard the whole thing. Just can't admit it to his little sister, that's all.

Anyway, all this was last season. *This* season he's a different guy. He goes to every match same as before, only he doesn't stand with the Ointment. He doesn't stand with me and Dad either, but that's all right. He's *grown,* see? Just like Barfax Town.

Activities

Additional support for teaching these book activities can be found at www.heinemann.co.uk/literature

The additional support resources contain:

- a full scheme of work: 32 medium-term lesson plans
- Student Sheets, Teacher's Notes and OHTs to accompany the lesson plans.

Humour

The Gnomecoming Party by Anne Fine

1   As you read this story, jot down quotations that create a strong visual image. Here are two to help you get started.

- 'It was like boot camp. Fresh commands kept hurtling over... Anything you've grown out of in this pile, please.' (page 1)

- 'And that is when I found him. I saw his pointy little cap first.' (page 1)

2   Find quotations to help you create a storyboard for this story, using a table like the one below. Try to find one quotation to use for each of the camera angles listed in the table.

Camera angle	Quotation
High-angled shot	
Low-angled shot	
Long shot	
Mid-shot	
Close up	
Extreme close up	
Two-person shot	
Over-the-shoulder shot	

3 Which moments in this story do you find amusing? Make a table like the one below, giving a brief summary of each moment, a quotation and a reason why it made you laugh.

Point (moment in the story)	Evidence (quotation from the story)	Explanation (why it made me laugh)
Mum telling James to tidy up	'Fresh commands kept hurtling over'	Sounds like he is in danger, with commands being personified as objects, which when thrown, could hurt.

4 Make a copy of the table below and note the key moments from the story, to show how the story is structured. Include a quotation from the story, to illustrate the change.

Stage of the story	Moment when the structure changes	Quotation from the story
Opening		
Development		
Complication		
Crisis		
Resolution		

More Bits of an Autobiography I May Not Write
by Morris Gleitzman

1 **a** List as many sitcoms as you can that are about families, such as *The Simpsons*, *My Family*.

    b What do these families have in common?

2 Read from 'I'll never forget when we got our first dog…' to '…I needed an extra six weeks.' (page 8)

    a How has the text been written?

    b What kind of text is this?

    c Describe the relationship between the writer and his children.

    d What tone has been used? How do you know this?

    e Find three examples of unusual vocabulary and sentence structure and say what is unusual about them.

    f Pick out four examples of humour. How they have been created?

3 Copy and complete the table below to show how the children feel about their father watching *The Bill*. One example has been put in for you.

The writer's words	What they show about the children's feelings
'…you promised you'd take us to the park.'	shows that he had already made a commitment and is breaking it; his children are reminding him of what he said
'"But Dad," they wailed'	
'"Suit yourself," said the kids, but if you don't get any exercise you will die.'	

4 Each section is organised in a similar way, for example:

- the writer does something wrong
- the children try to help
- the problem is sorted out.

Copy and complete the table below to show how the writer has used this structure.

	Section 1: Dog-walking	Section 2: Bushfire	Section 3: The dog vs *The Bill*
The writer does something wrong			
The children try to help			
The problem is sorted out			

Brave New Words

Schooldays by Bill Bryson

1 Read from: 'Greenwood, my elementary school, was a wonderful old building...' (page 16) to '...every girl they asked remembered that they had worn galoshes in third grade.' (page 20)

2 Find and write down examples of the following that have been used to start a sentence:

   - a connective
   - an adverb (-ly)
   - proper noun (specific person, place or thing)
   - present participle verb (-ing)
   - question word (wh...?).

3 Find and write down examples of the following:

   - simile (using 'as' or 'like' to make a comparison)
   - metaphor (a comparison where something is compared to something else)
   - noun phrase (noun + adjectives to expand description e.g. 'wonderful old building')
   - superlative (words ending in -est e.g. scariest)
   - connective linking ideas and paragraphs
   - use of humour
   - exaggeration.

4 Now read the rest of 'Schooldays'. Imagine that the author intended to give each anecdote a subheading, but forgot. Give each anecdote a subheading; you could use a short phrase from the text, for example 'The wonderful old building'.

5 Select ten funny moments from 'Schooldays'. Try and select a quotation for each one.

6   Plot your ten funny moments on a humour graph like the one below. On the vertical axis, record how funny you found each moment, on the horizontal axis are the moments (you could use a key A–J, with the moments described underneath.)

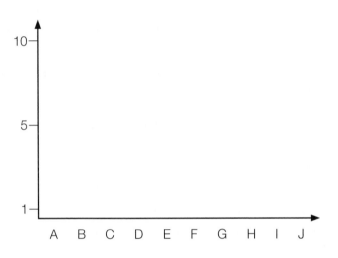

Mrs Bixby and the Colonel's Coat by Roald Dahl

Read the story, then answer the questions. (The activities can be used with any story.)

Genre (type of story, e.g. diary, humour, historical, sporting)

1   What clues can you find to indicate the genre of this story?
2   Are the characters stereotypical (what you would expect)?
3   How does the vocabulary indicate the genre? List three phrases that tell you the genre.

Structure (how a piece of writing is put together)

1   How are the characters introduced? (Speech, actions, by other characters, by the narrator.)
2   What is mentioned that indicates that the plot will develop?
3   What devices has the author used to hook the reader?
4   Is there a twist at the end? If so, what is it?

Setting (where the story is set)

1   Where is the story set? (If there is more than one location, list them all.)
2   Draw a sketch to illustrate each setting from the story.
3   Write quotations around your picture to support your interpretation.

Characters (the people in the story)

1   Draw a picture of each character in the story.
2   Around each picture, write five adjectives to describe that character.
3   Select at least one quotation for each character.

Atmosphere (a feeling or mood given by the surroundings)

1 Draw a timeline and plot the events of the story.

2 What is the atmosphere at the start of the story?

3 Pick out moments when the atmosphere changes.

4 Explain why and how these changes occur.

Language (how the writer has used words and sentences)

1 How does the story open?

2 Select five interesting sentences and say why you chose each one.

3 Find a simile or a metaphor. Why has the author made this comparison?

Copy and complete the table below.

Narrative devices	Quotations and explanations
Perspective: 1st, 3rd person? Give an example	
Background: What information is given? How is it relevant?	
Clues: What information is the reader given for the creation of the plot?	
Build-up of tension: How is tension created?	
Climax: What is the main moment of the story?	
Twists: Describe any unexpected events.	

History

A Place on the Piano by Eva Ibbotson

1   Read the story as far as the words '…brought up with peasants.'
    (page 54). Try to make at least three predictions about the rest
    of the story. Write them in a table like the one below.

Point (your prediction)	Evidence (words from the story that support your prediction)	Explanation (why this might happen; what effect this might have on the rest of the story)
The little girl they find will not be the one they expect.	'Wars are expensive'	Her family can't afford to feed her, so they decide to send her to England, even though she is the wrong girl.

2   Find quotations on as many of the points in the diagram below
    as you can. If the text is not explicit, say what you think, for
    example if a character's appearance is not described, say
    how you imagine it. You could write about Michael, Michael's
    mother, Mrs Glossop, Marianne or Mrs Wasilewski.

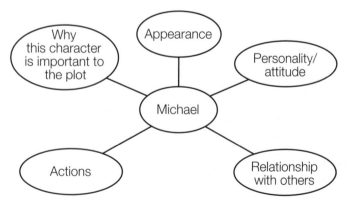

3 Select at least five quotations that you think you could illustrate, for example:

- 'Marianne had been thrown out of a cattle train when she was a baby.' (page 53)

- 'Their house was the largest in the square, double-fronted – and furnished as though the war had never been.' (page 55)

4 What clues does the author give to explain why Michael's mother lies about Marianne? Do you think Michael's mother was right to do this? Give reasons for your opinion.

The Daughter by Jacqueline Wilson

1 Get into groups; each group should take a different question from the list below, and should be prepared to present their answers to the rest of the class.

    a Are you superstitious? How? Why?

    b Do you believe in witches? Why?

    c Do you think children can be 'evil'? Why?

    d Why might people abuse children?

2 Make brief notes to answer each of the questions below. For each one, find two quotations from the story to support your answer, then explain your opinion.

    a Are the characters in this story superstitious?

    b Do the different characters in this story believe in witches?

    c How do you think the daughter is thought of by her father?

    d What evidence is there that the daughter is abused?

3 Copy and complete the table below by explaining which literary device the author has used and why she might have used it.

Quotation	Which literary device is this?	Why has it been used?
'Turn and turn and turn.'		
'My father is very flushed, very fuddled.'		
'Is it my mother?'		

4 Below are three responses to the story. Write out the one that you think is the strongest message behind 'The Daughter', then write two sentences explaining your choice.

   a During the sixteenth century there were superstitions about girls.

   b During the sixteenth century girls did not have equal status with boys.

   c During the sixteenth century people believed in witches.

I think this is the strongest message behind the story 'The Daughter' because …

The Princess Spy by Jamila Gavin

1   What do you associate with the word 'heroine'?

2   Find four sentences that show that Princess Noor Inayat Khan was a heroine.

3   Find three sentences that provide evidence of the setting and historical context.

4   Copy and complete the figurative language chart below, finding four similes or metaphors that are used in the story.

Simile or metaphor?	Quotation	What is being compared to what and why?
Simile	'a flurry of princesses surround me like swans'	The princesses are being compared to swans, this might be because they are flapping their arms like wings. Swans are also regal animals.

Real Tears by Celia Rees

1 Think about the title of this story, and make at least three predictions about what might happen in it. Now read the story. Were any of your predictions right?

2 Describe the kind of reception that a soldier might receive when he comes home on leave from Iraq. Use as wide a variety of adjectives as you can.

3 Find quotations that show the other characters' attitudes towards Ben. Draw a spider diagram like the one below and add at least one quotation for each character.

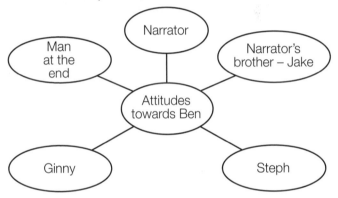

4 Make a table like the one below and list at least three advantages and three disadvantages of joining the British Army.

Advantages of joining the British Army	Disadvantages of joining the British Army
1.	1.
2.	2.
3.	3.

5 Why do you think the author wrote this story? What was she trying to make us think about?

6 Consider your first responses when thinking about the following questions:

   a How did the ending make you feel?

   b What did the ending make you think about?

   c Why might the author have ended her story in this way?

Diaries

Worth It by Malorie Blackman

1 Copy the table below and complete it as you read the story.

KWEL (Know, Want, Evidence, Learnt)	
Read the first entry: Monday 28th June, then answer the following questions	
What do I **know** about this person from their diary?	
What do I **want** to know about this person?	
Where will I find the **evidence** for this?	
Continue reading the diary, then answer the next question	
What have I **learnt** about Judith?	

2 Find and write down sentences that use examples of the following punctuation:

   ?   **!**   **...**   **' '**   **-**

3 Give three reasons why it is important for a writer to use a variety of punctuation.

4 Copy and complete the table below.

Literary devices	Example from the story	Why the author has used this device
Rhetorical question A question posed for effect rather than for the purpose of getting an answer		
Exaggerate To represent something as greater than it is; to overstate		

Activities

Literary devices	Example from the story	Why the author has used this device
Italicise To print in *italics*; to change (characters, words, etc. in normal typeface) to *italics*		
Repetition Where words or certain phrases are repeated for greater emphasis		
Emotive language Language that causes an emotional response in people		

The Princess Diaries by Meg Cabot

1 When you read a text, you may find some new or unfamiliar words. The words in this list are a mixture of new vocabulary and Americanisms. Look them up in a dictionary and write their meanings in your own copy of the list.

Word	Definition	Word	Definition
repressing		mandatory	
flunking		incarcerated	
solitary		omnipotent	
diversity		concierge	
prank		scepticism	

2 Create Mia's profile, based on your reading of 'The Princess Diaries'.

Name_____ Nickname _____

Age _____ Born _____

Hobbies _____

Heroes _____

What Mia might be when she grows up _____

Personality at the moment _____

Worries _____

Physical makeup _____

Height _____ Weight _____

Hair colour _____ Eye colour _____

Distinguishing marks _____

Best friend_____ Sex _____ Age _____

Personality _____

Pets _____ Name _____ Age _____

Mia's house _____

Mia's room _____

Other important information _____

3 Using the same or slightly adapted headings, create your own profile.

4 Compare 'Worth It' with 'The Princess Diaries'. You could compare content, theme, plot, characters and message.

Julie and Me and Michael Owen Makes Three by Alan Gibbons

1 Copy and complete the table below to analyse Terry's reaction when he sees Julie for the first time. Your table should have one row for each of five different adjectives.

Point (Terry's reaction)	Evidence (a quote to support this point)	Explanation (Which device has been used? Why has Terry's reaction been described in this way?)
Nervous	'I've gone all gaspy and urgent and breathless…'	Cluster of three to emphasise Terry's growing nervousness

2 Read the 7.30pm entry and focus on the description of the football match (pages 144–8). Select ten verbs (remember: a verb is a word that expresses the idea of action, happening, or being).

3 Order the events in the story. Copy the table below and write the numbers 1–14 against the events, in the order in which they occur in the story.

Event	1–14
a Bobby is popular and has no trouble speaking to girls.	
b Bobby, Terry and his father discuss the football, before it starts.	
c England is winning and the score is 2–1.	
d Kelly catches Terry staring at Julie and calls him 'Freak-a-zoid'.	
e Phil Neville fouls the Romanian player.	
f Romania equalise, the score is 2–2.	
g Terry discovers that Julie supports Liverpool Football Club.	

Activities

Event	1–14
h Terry invites Bobby to watch the England versus Romania football game.	
i Terry recaps on Tuesday 20 June 2000.	
j Terry remembers David Beckham's foul in the World Cup game.	
k Terry sees Julie for the first time.	
l Terry thinks about the trip to Alton Towers.	
m Terry worries that Julie may be a 'bimbo'.	
n Terry's Dad, Geoff, becomes angry and tells his son that he is moving out.	

Double Thirteen by Eleanor Updale

1   Why do you think the narrator is having a bad day? Give at least two reasons.

2   Comment on the language used in the following sentence: 'I mean, he practises *at lunchtime*.' (page 166). Explain why the author has used italics here.

3   Find an example of a one-word sentence. Why might the author have used it?

4   Select a quotation to mark each of the different parts of the story. Write your quotations in a copy of the table below.

Part of story	Words that mark the different parts of the story
Opening	
Development	
Complications	
Crisis	
Resolution	

Sport

Left Foot Forward by Jan Mark

1 As you read the story, pay particular attention to the first word of each paragraph.

   a Select five interesting opening sentences of paragraphs and write them in your own copy of the table below.

   b For each paragraph, write down a word that you think gives a good indication of what that paragraph was about. (Look up unfamiliar words in a dictionary.)

   c Briefly summarise what the paragraph is about.

Paragraph-opening sentence	What does the chosen word imply?	What was the paragraph about?

2 Which of the following are quotations?

   a Shaun was really observant, he noticed people.

   b 'The other two left-footers planned to bring along computer games next time.'

   c '…Shaun had sole possession of the ball, which was no longer round but lopsided, like the gibbous moon.'

   d Shaun was so excited it felt like someone had punched him in the ribs.

   e Miss Stevens was offering Shaun support, he knew he should accept it.

   f 'Enthusiasm…important attitude…essential to team spirit…'

3 Ellipsis (…) is a piece of punctuation. It can be used to indicate:

a Words at the start of a sentence that are not being quoted.

b Words that are left out in a quote.

c That tension is being created as the sentence is not finished.

When ellipsis is used, the sentence still needs to make grammatical sense.

Look again at **c** and **f** in question 2. Why have ellipses been used here?

4 **a** Draw or search for suitable pictures, using the Internet, to illustrate Shaun, Mr Dunkin and Mr Prior.

    b Find and select at least three quotations about each of these characters and write them around your pictures. Don't forget to include speech marks around your quotes.

    c Under each quotation, add at least one adjective that describes that character. Try using a thesaurus to help you find and use a word you didn't know before.

The Jump by Anthony Masters

1   As you read the story, find quotations on the themes named
    in the spider diagram below. You could note them in one
    large spider diagram, or in separate spider diagrams (one per
    theme.)

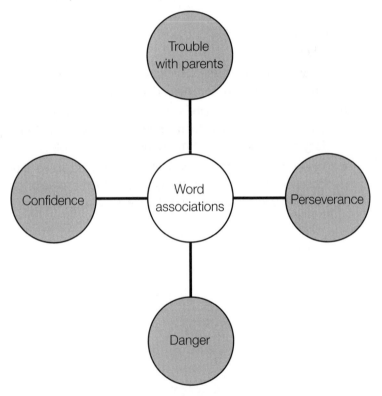

2   Compare 'The Jump' and 'Left Foot Forward', using a Venn
    diagram like the one opposite.

    Think about: content, themes, plot, characters, message.
    The ideas you write in the overlapping area are the points for
    comparison.

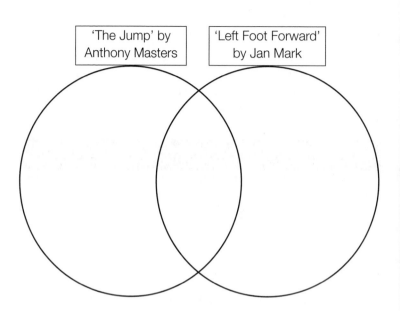

'The Jump' by
Anthony Masters

'Left Foot Forward'
by Jan Mark

3 Write your comparison, using full sentences and paragraphs. The following connectives for comparison and contrast could help you: *both*, *equally*, *similarly*, *in the same way*, *likewise*, *like*, *as with*. Useful connectives for contrast include: *alternatively*, *whereas*, *instead*, *otherwise*, *unlike*, *on the other hand*.

No Sweat by Michelle Magorian

1 Have you ever changed your views about someone? Before you read this story, think about two occasions when your attitudes to someone have changed. Copy and complete the table below, exploring and explaining the change in your attitudes.

Your attitude before	Why your attitude changed	Your attitude afterwards
I felt that X didn't like me	I realised that this was because they did not know me	I decided that X was a friendly person after all

2 Now read the story 'No Sweat'.

3 a How does Mark feel towards Joan at the **start** of the story? Write notes to show what you find, and add quotations from the story that show this, for example:

Mark's attitude towards Joan at the start of the story is one of disrespect:
- 'he was going to be swimming next to a bunch of wrinklies!'.

b Describe Mark's attitude and feelings towards his friends Jacko and Terry at the **start** and the **end** of the story. Write your answer in the same 'notes and quotations' format that you used in part **a** of this question.

4 Chart ten events that occur during Mark's swim and think about how he is feeling at those moments. If you can, give a brief reason and explain why Mark might be feeling this way.

Events using a quotation	Mark's feelings
1 'Mark walked out of the men's changing room to the big pool.'	Nervous about swimming two hundred lengths
2	

5 How might this range of feelings link to possible messages behind 'No Sweat'? What messages could this story be commmunicating to the reader?

Going Up by Robert Swindells

1 Read the first five paragraphs of the story and make at least three predictions about what might happen later. Find a quotation from the story to support each of your predictions, and explain:

a why you think this might happen

b the effect this event could have on the story.

Record your ideas in a table like the one below.

Point (your prediction)	Evidence (words from the story that support your prediction)	Explanation (why this might happen; the effect this might have on the rest of the story)

2 How do we know that Dale is reluctant to take Terry to the match? Make a copy of the table below and fill in quotations to support your decision.

Statement	yes ✔ no ✗	Quotation – evidence from the story to show why you put a tick or a cross
a) Dale does not like football		
b) Dale is angry about being told what to do		
c) Dale does not want to be laughed at by his friends		
d) Dale does not feel old enough to be responsible for Terry		
e) Dale is worried about what will happen after the match		

3 Give two reasons why the following sentence is effective: 'A guy charged over a sea of broken glass, aimed a kick at a youth in the doorway and the pair of them swayed snarling out of sight.' (page 215).

4 What do you think the moral of the story could be? Try to give at least three reasons for your answer.